IDENTITY

A STORY OF
TRANSITIONING

Written by **COREY MAISON**

Art, Ink, Colors and Lettering by
FANTOONS ANIMATION STUDIOS

Zuiker Press

Los Angeles

IDENTITY: A STORY OF TRANSITIONING

Corey Maison Photographs © 2020 Corey Maison
Cover photo courtesy Anna Neubauer

Written by Anthony E. Zuiker
Art, Ink, Colors and Lettering by Fantoons Animation Studios
Designed by Roberta Melzl
Edited by Rob Tokar

Founders: Michelle & Anthony E. Zuiker
Publisher: David Wilk

Published by Zuiker Press
16255 Ventura Blvd.
Suite #900
Encino, CA 91436
United States of America

Visit us online at www.zuikerpress.com

ISBN 978-1-947378-24-7 (hardcover)
ISBN 978-1-947378-26-1 (eBook)

PRINTED IN CANADA
September 2020
10 9 8 7 6 5 4 3 2 1

DEDICATED TO ... every young person who needs to be reminded they are not alone.

HOPE lies within these pages.

ZUIKER PRESS

... is a husband and wife publishing company that champions the voices of young authors. We are an **ISSUE-BASED** literary house. All of our authors have elected to tell their personal stories and be ambassadors of their cause. Their goal, as is ours, is that young people will learn from their pain and heroics and find **HOPE**, **CHANGE**, and **HAPPINESS** in their own lives.

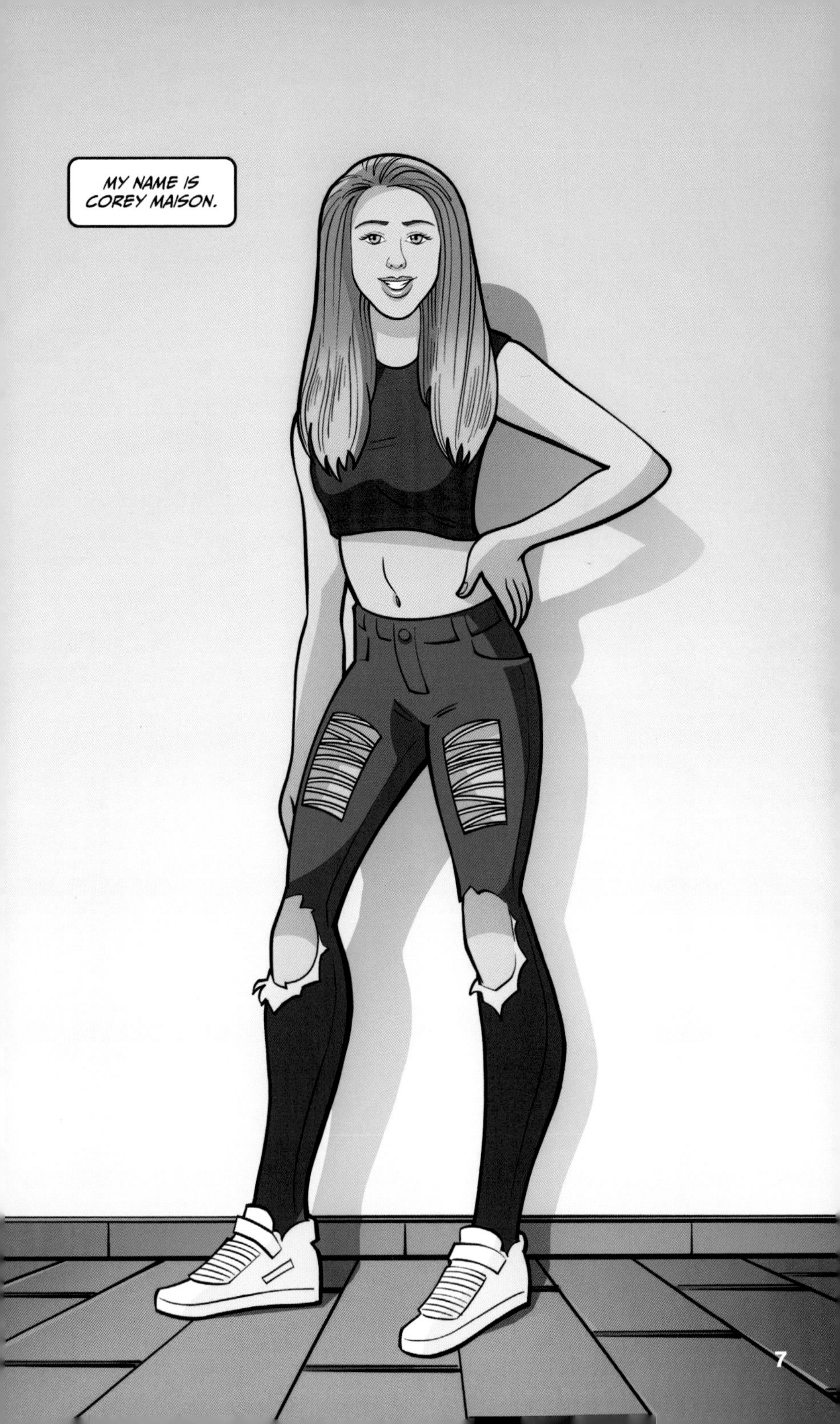
MY NAME IS COREY MAISON.

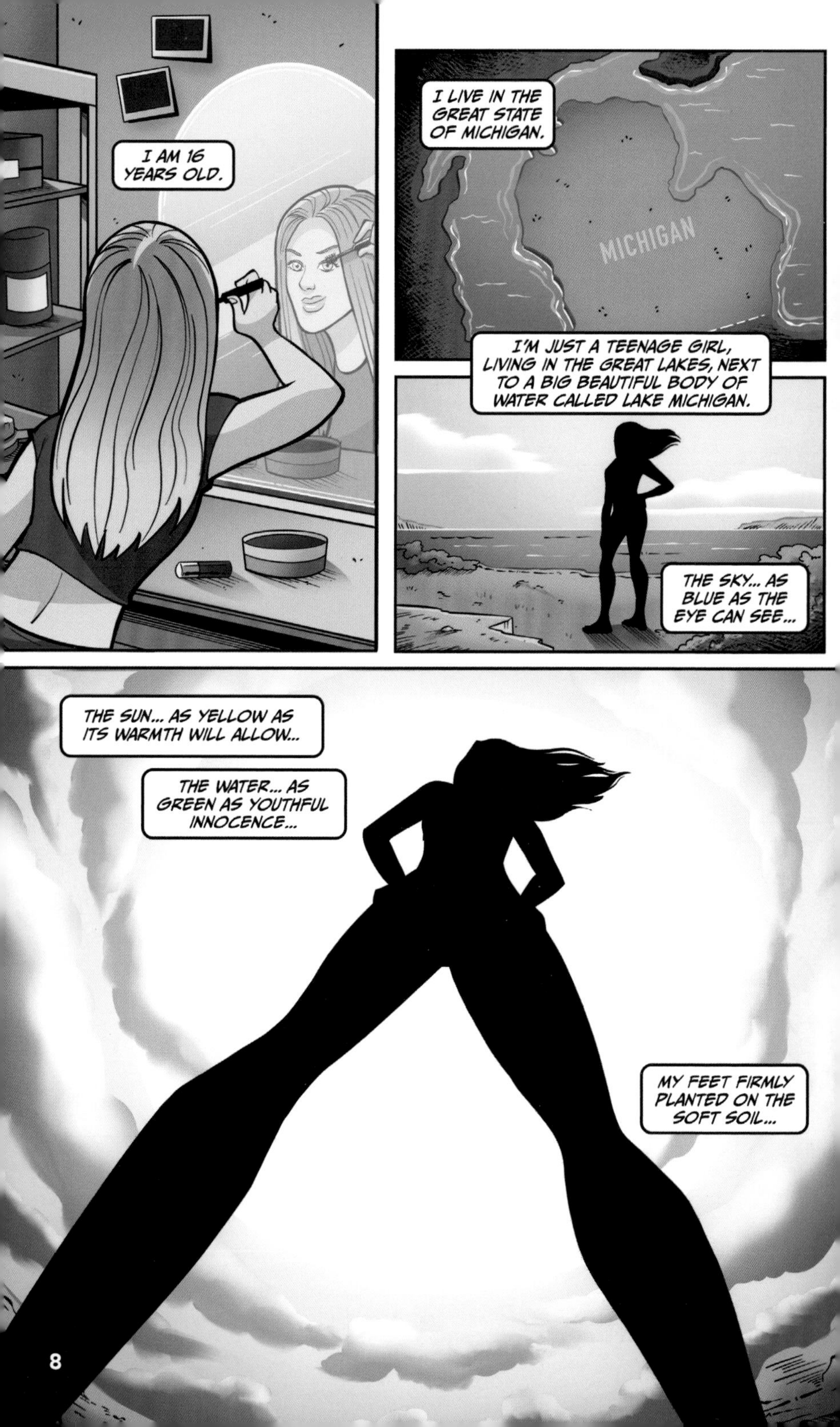

I AM 16 YEARS OLD.
I LIVE IN THE GREAT STATE OF MICHIGAN.
MICHIGAN
I'M JUST A TEENAGE GIRL, LIVING IN THE GREAT LAKES, NEXT TO A BIG BEAUTIFUL BODY OF WATER CALLED LAKE MICHIGAN.
THE SKY... AS BLUE AS THE EYE CAN SEE...
THE SUN... AS YELLOW AS ITS WARMTH WILL ALLOW...
THE WATER... AS GREEN AS YOUTHFUL INNOCENCE...
MY FEET FIRMLY PLANTED ON THE SOFT SOIL...

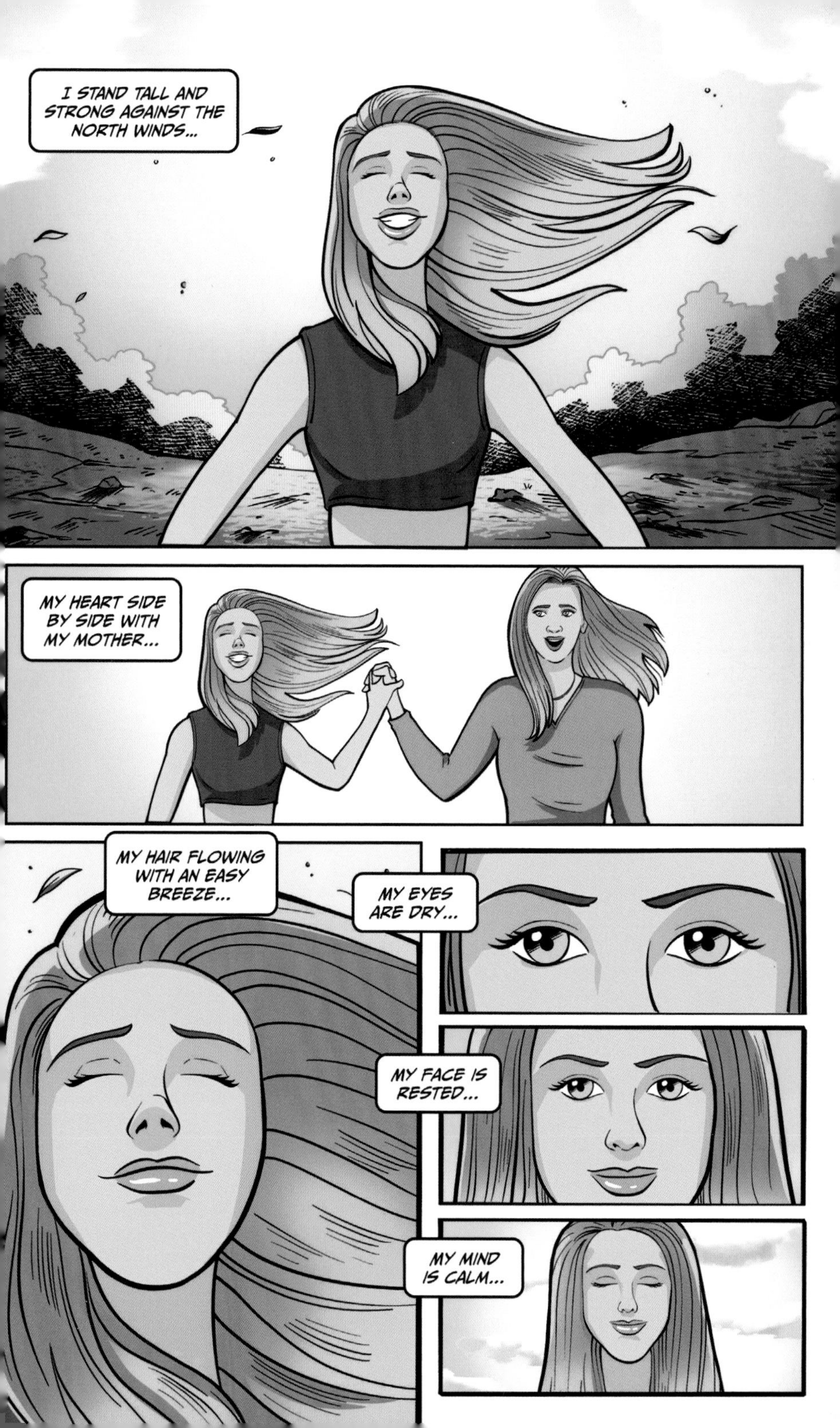
I STAND TALL AND STRONG AGAINST THE NORTH WINDS...
MY HEART SIDE BY SIDE WITH MY MOTHER...
MY HAIR FLOWING WITH AN EASY BREEZE...
MY EYES ARE DRY...
MY FACE IS RESTED...
MY MIND IS CALM...

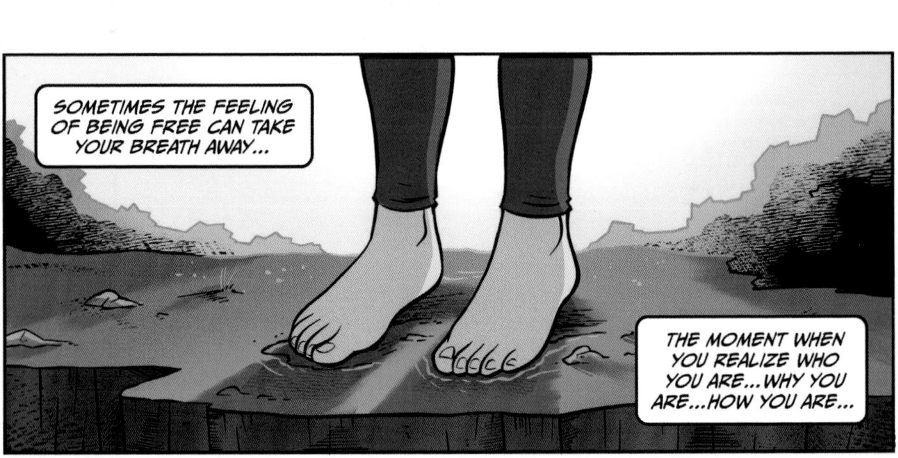
SOMETIMES THE FEELING OF BEING FREE CAN TAKE YOUR BREATH AWAY...
THE MOMENT WHEN YOU REALIZE WHO YOU ARE...WHY YOU ARE...HOW YOU ARE...

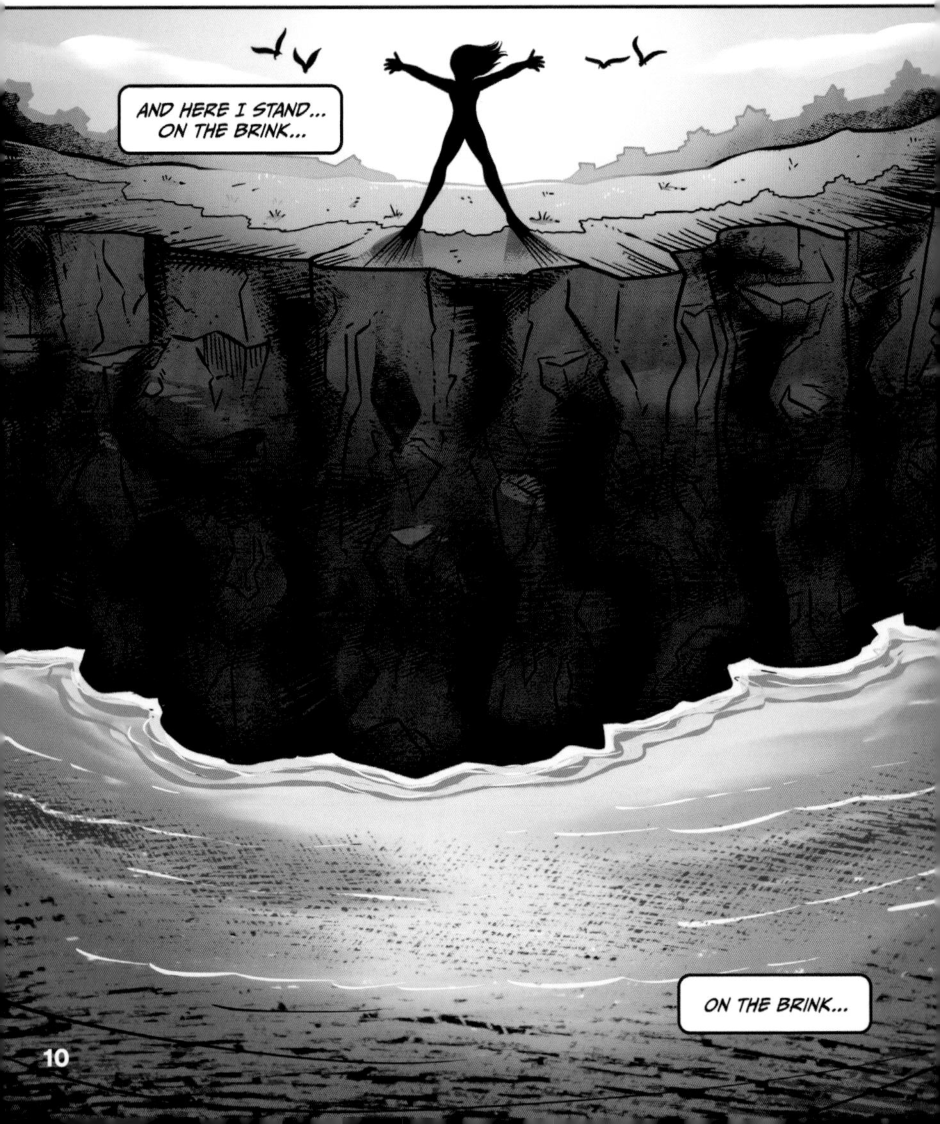
AND HERE I STAND... ON THE BRINK...
ON THE BRINK...

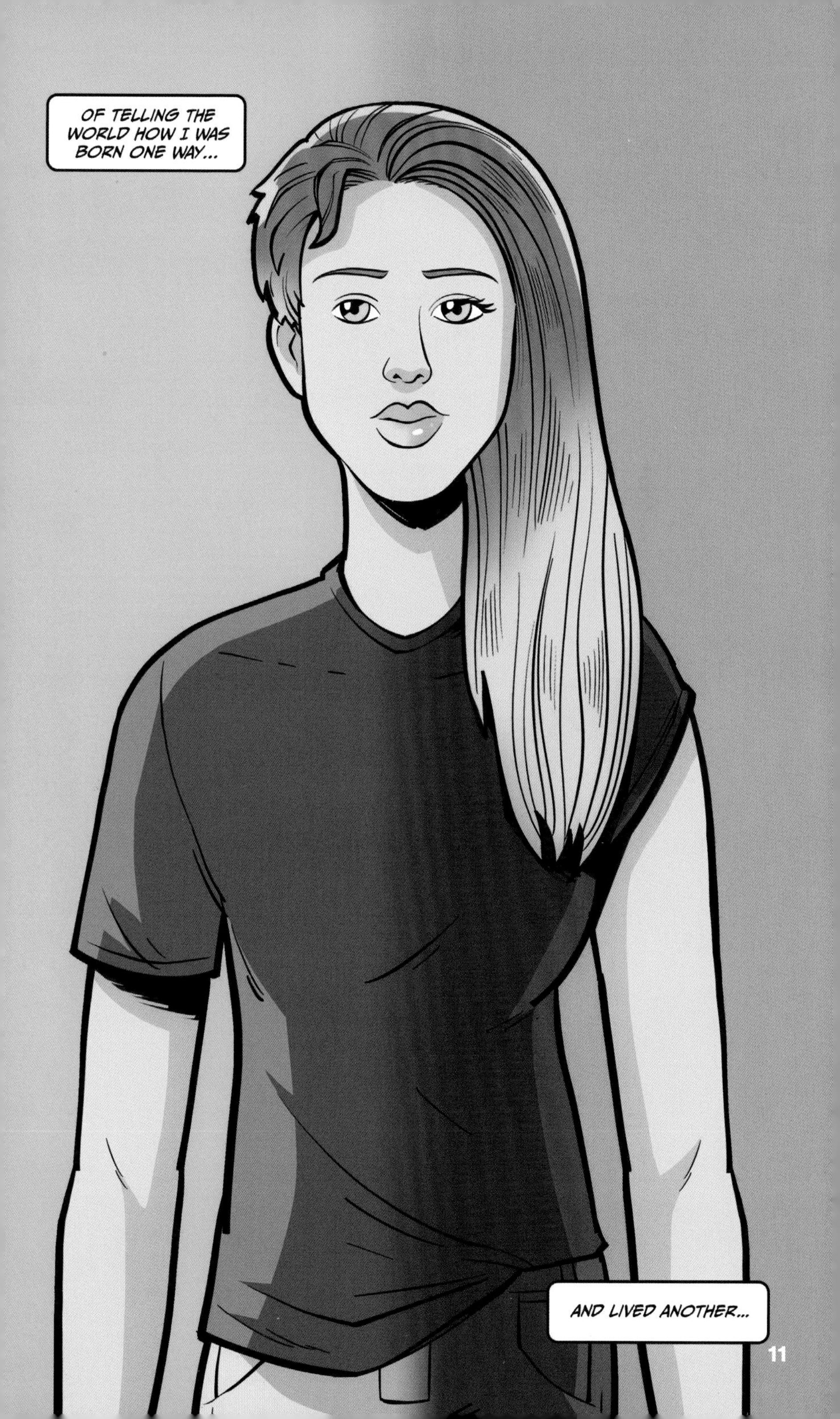
OF TELLING THE WORLD HOW I WAS BORN ONE WAY...
AND LIVED ANOTHER...

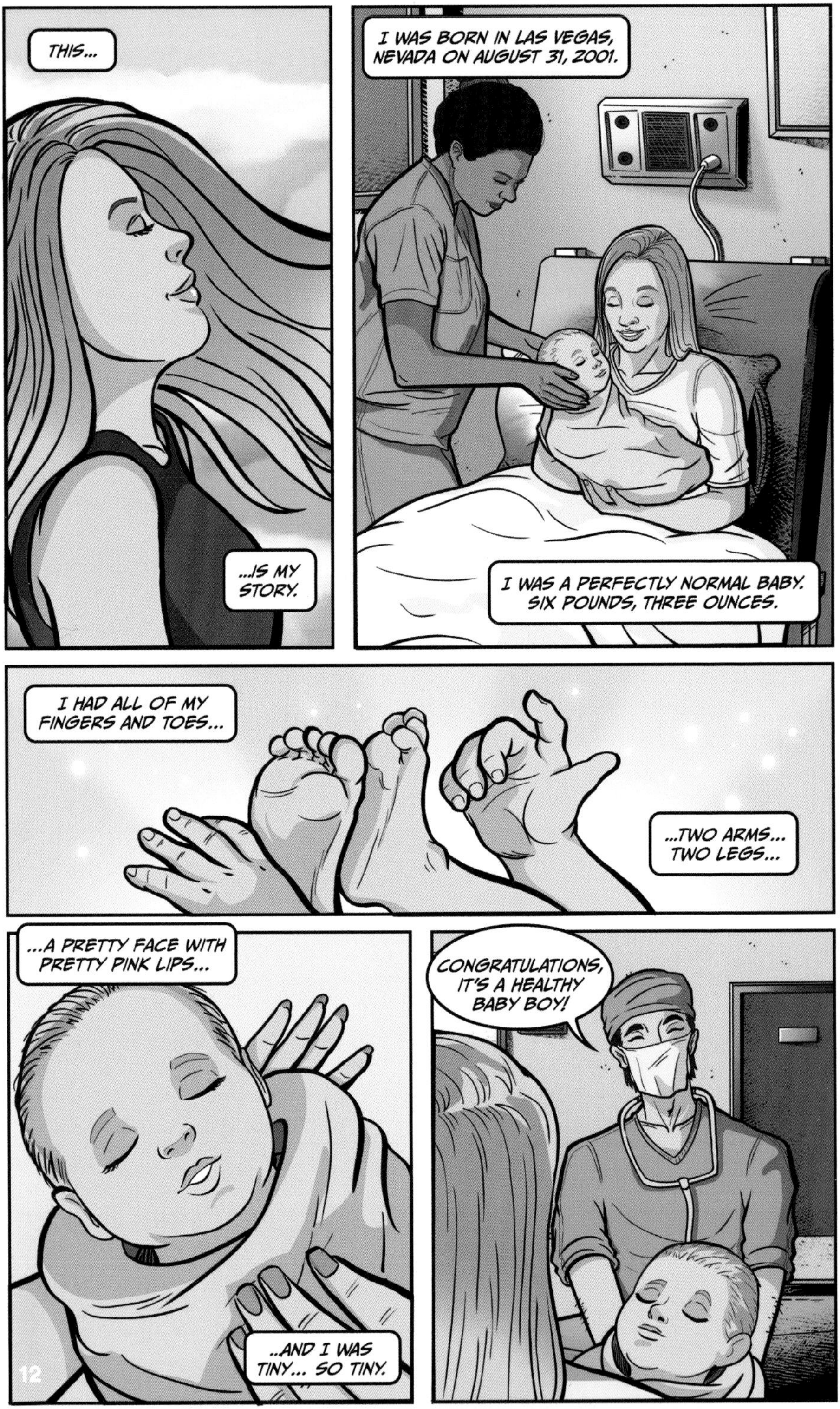
THIS...
...IS MY STORY.
I WAS BORN IN LAS VEGAS, NEVADA ON AUGUST 31, 2001.
I WAS A PERFECTLY NORMAL BABY. SIX POUNDS, THREE OUNCES.
I HAD ALL OF MY FINGERS AND TOES...
...TWO ARMS... TWO LEGS...
...A PRETTY FACE WITH PRETTY PINK LIPS...
..AND I WAS TINY... SO TINY.
CONGRATULATIONS, IT'S A HEALTHY BABY BOY!

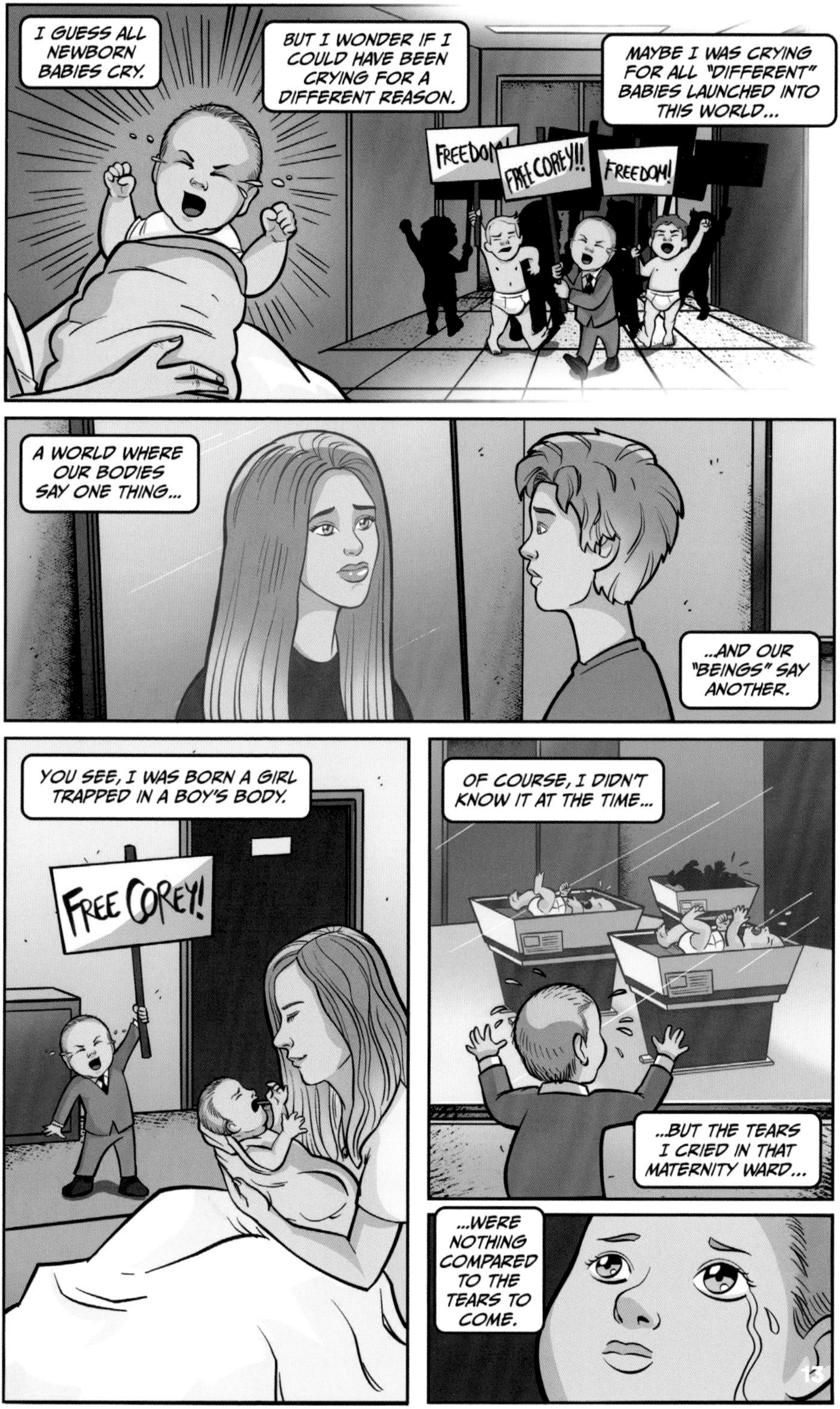

I GUESS ALL NEWBORN BABIES CRY.
BUT I WONDER IF I COULD HAVE BEEN CRYING FOR A DIFFERENT REASON.
MAYBE I WAS CRYING FOR ALL "DIFFERENT" BABIES LAUNCHED INTO THIS WORLD...
FREEDOM!
FREE COREY!!
FREEDOM!
A WORLD WHERE OUR BODIES SAY ONE THING...
...AND OUR "BEINGS" SAY ANOTHER.
YOU SEE, I WAS BORN A GIRL TRAPPED IN A BOY'S BODY.
FREE COREY!
OF COURSE, I DIDN'T KNOW IT AT THE TIME...
...BUT THE TEARS I CRIED IN THAT MATERNITY WARD...
...WERE NOTHING COMPARED TO THE TEARS TO COME.
13

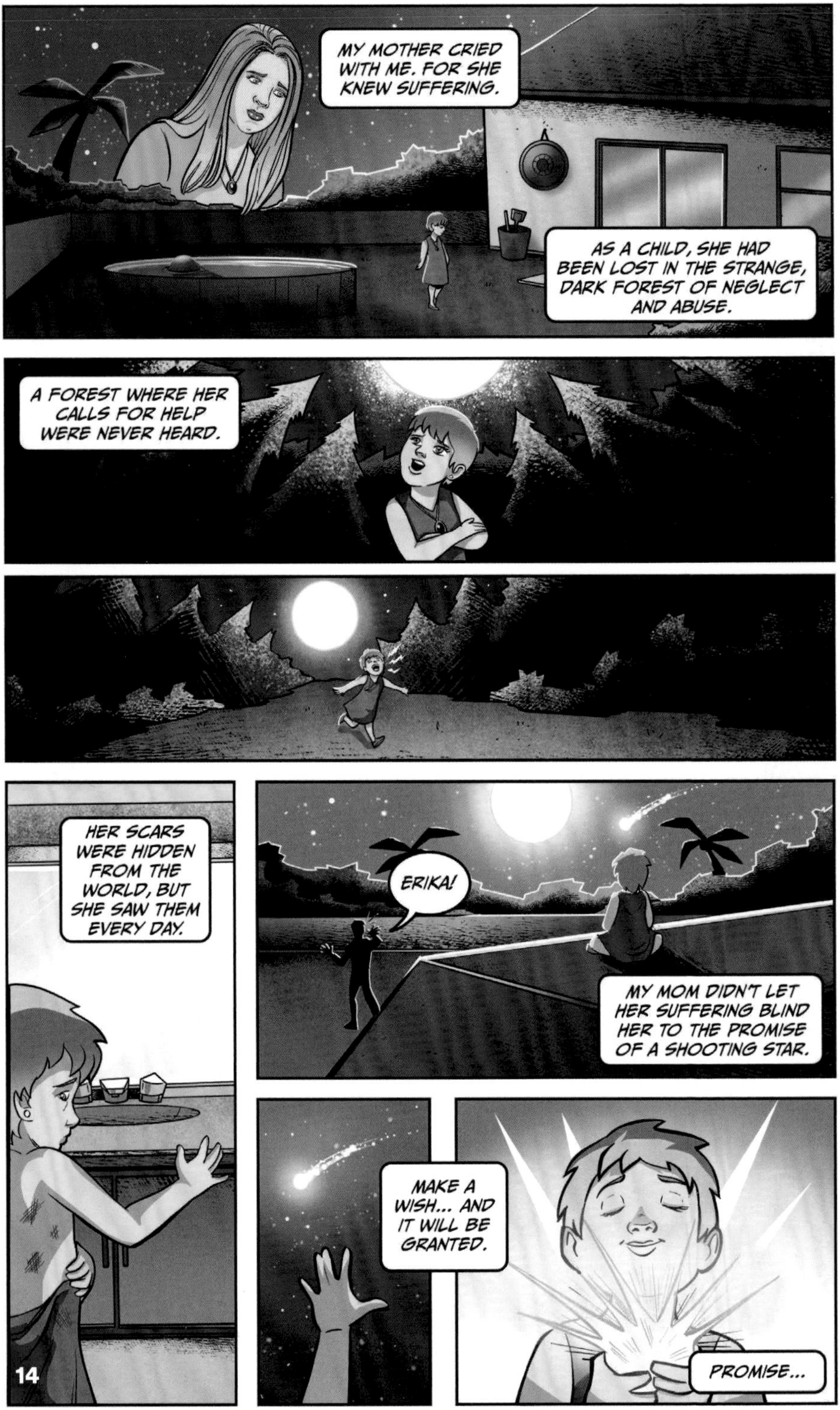
MY MOTHER CRIED WITH ME. FOR SHE KNEW SUFFERING.
AS A CHILD, SHE HAD BEEN LOST IN THE STRANGE, DARK FOREST OF NEGLECT AND ABUSE.
A FOREST WHERE HER CALLS FOR HELP WERE NEVER HEARD.
HER SCARS WERE HIDDEN FROM THE WORLD, BUT SHE SAW THEM EVERY DAY.
ERIKA!
MY MOM DIDN'T LET HER SUFFERING BLIND HER TO THE PROMISE OF A SHOOTING STAR.
MAKE A WISH... AND IT WILL BE GRANTED.
PROMISE...

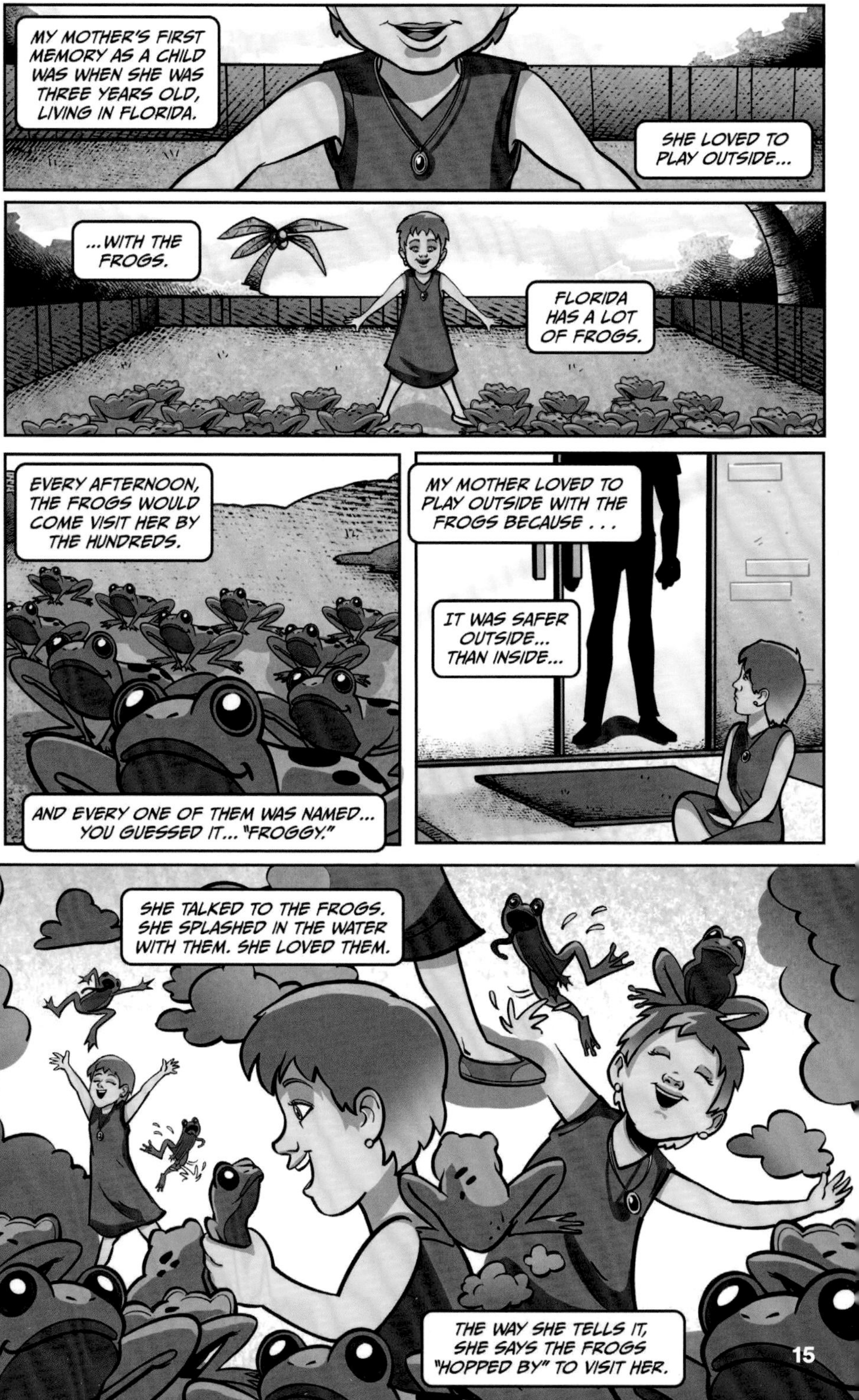

MY MOTHER'S FIRST MEMORY AS A CHILD WAS WHEN SHE WAS THREE YEARS OLD, LIVING IN FLORIDA.
SHE LOVED TO PLAY OUTSIDE...
...WITH THE FROGS.
FLORIDA HAS A LOT OF FROGS.
EVERY AFTERNOON, THE FROGS WOULD COME VISIT HER BY THE HUNDREDS.
AND EVERY ONE OF THEM WAS NAMED... YOU GUESSED IT... "FROGGY."
MY MOTHER LOVED TO PLAY OUTSIDE WITH THE FROGS BECAUSE . . .
IT WAS SAFER OUTSIDE... THAN INSIDE...
SHE TALKED TO THE FROGS. SHE SPLASHED IN THE WATER WITH THEM. SHE LOVED THEM.
THE WAY SHE TELLS IT, SHE SAYS THE FROGS "HOPPED BY" TO VISIT HER.

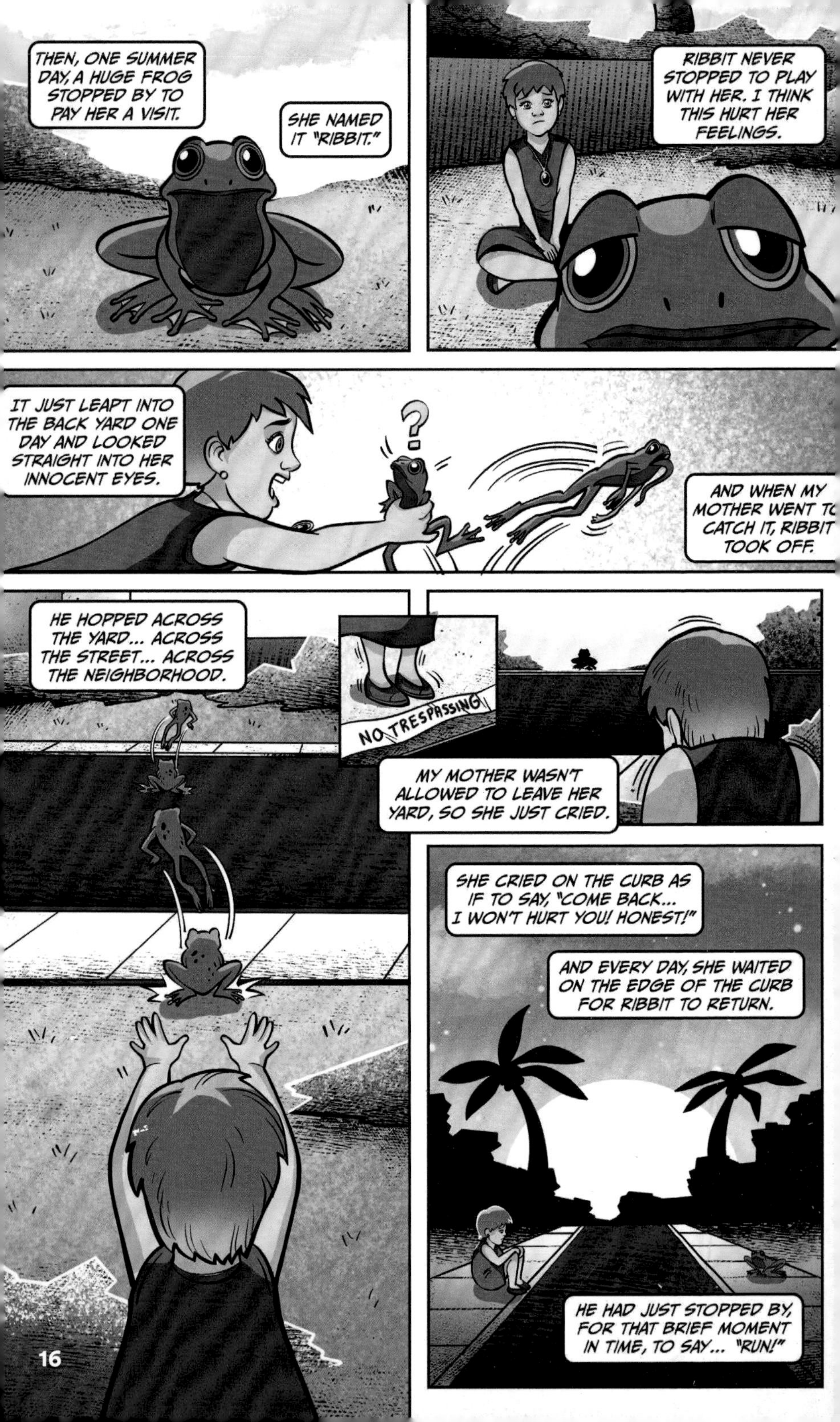

THEN, ONE SUMMER DAY, A HUGE FROG STOPPED BY TO PAY HER A VISIT.
SHE NAMED IT "RIBBIT."
RIBBIT NEVER STOPPED TO PLAY WITH HER. I THINK THIS HURT HER FEELINGS.
IT JUST LEAPT INTO THE BACK YARD ONE DAY AND LOOKED STRAIGHT INTO HER INNOCENT EYES.
?
AND WHEN MY MOTHER WENT TO CATCH IT, RIBBIT TOOK OFF.
HE HOPPED ACROSS THE YARD... ACROSS THE STREET... ACROSS THE NEIGHBORHOOD.
NO TRESPASSING
MY MOTHER WASN'T ALLOWED TO LEAVE HER YARD, SO SHE JUST CRIED.
SHE CRIED ON THE CURB AS IF TO SAY, "COME BACK... I WON'T HURT YOU! HONEST!"
AND EVERY DAY, SHE WAITED ON THE EDGE OF THE CURB FOR RIBBIT TO RETURN.
HE HAD JUST STOPPED BY, FOR THAT BRIEF MOMENT IN TIME, TO SAY... "RUN!"

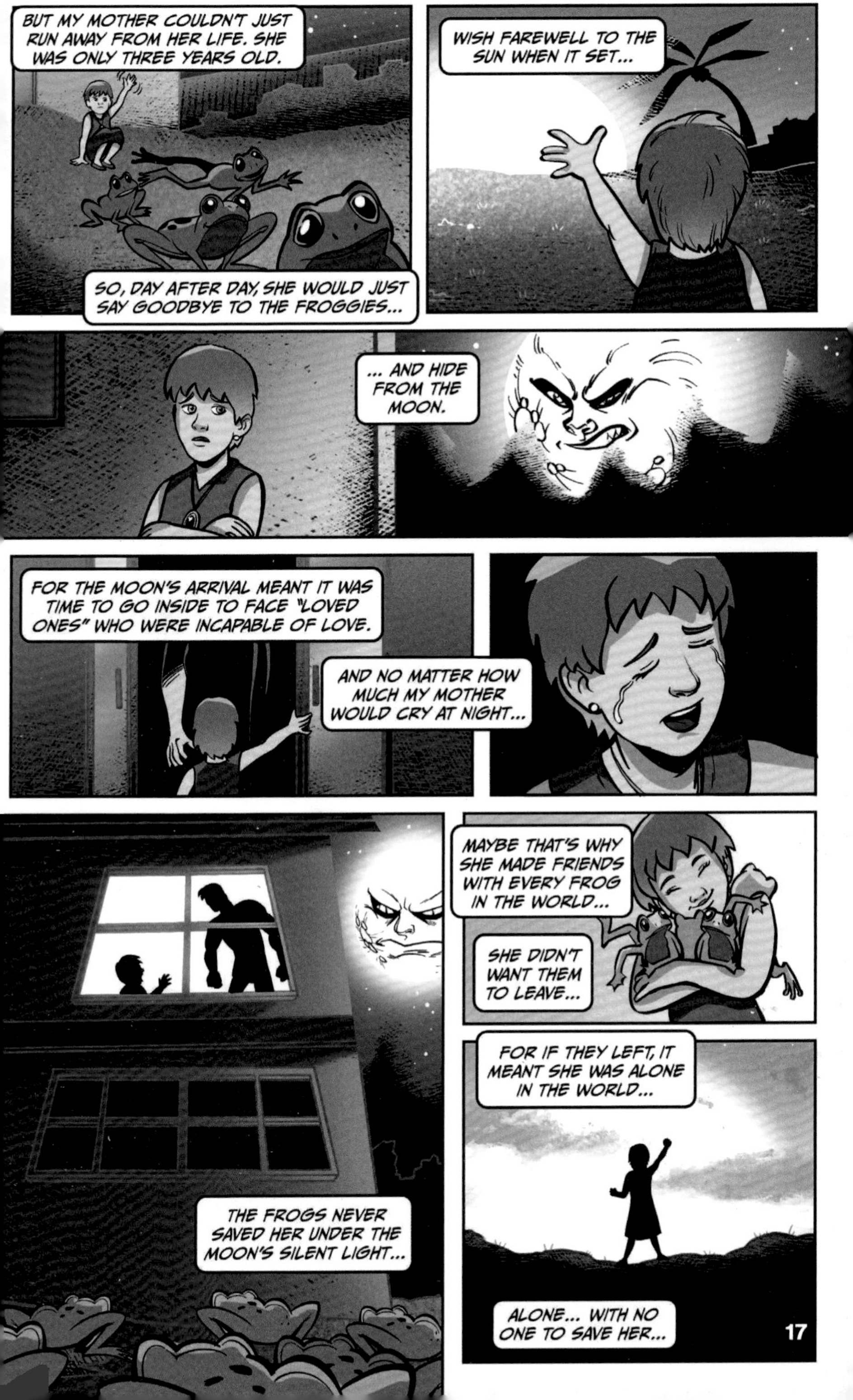
BUT MY MOTHER COULDN'T JUST RUN AWAY FROM HER LIFE. SHE WAS ONLY THREE YEARS OLD.
SO, DAY AFTER DAY, SHE WOULD JUST SAY GOODBYE TO THE FROGGIES...
WISH FAREWELL TO THE SUN WHEN IT SET...
... AND HIDE FROM THE MOON.
FOR THE MOON'S ARRIVAL MEANT IT WAS TIME TO GO INSIDE TO FACE "LOVED ONES" WHO WERE INCAPABLE OF LOVE.
AND NO MATTER HOW MUCH MY MOTHER WOULD CRY AT NIGHT...
THE FROGS NEVER SAVED HER UNDER THE MOON'S SILENT LIGHT...
MAYBE THAT'S WHY SHE MADE FRIENDS WITH EVERY FROG IN THE WORLD...
SHE DIDN'T WANT THEM TO LEAVE...
FOR IF THEY LEFT, IT MEANT SHE WAS ALONE IN THE WORLD...
ALONE... WITH NO ONE TO SAVE HER...

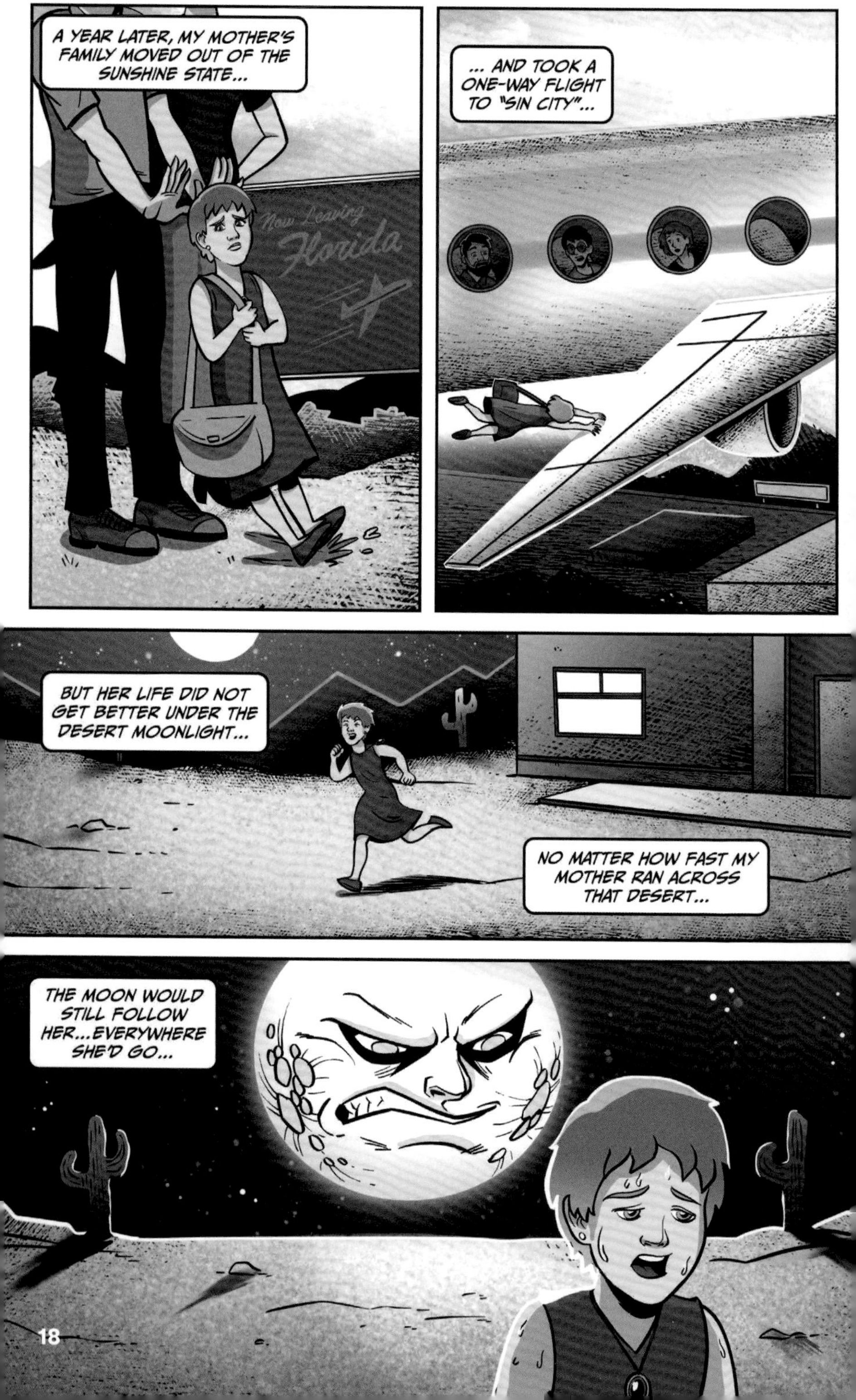
A YEAR LATER, MY MOTHER'S FAMILY MOVED OUT OF THE SUNSHINE STATE...
Now Leaving Florida
... AND TOOK A ONE-WAY FLIGHT TO "SIN CITY"...
BUT HER LIFE DID NOT GET BETTER UNDER THE DESERT MOONLIGHT...
NO MATTER HOW FAST MY MOTHER RAN ACROSS THAT DESERT...
THE MOON WOULD STILL FOLLOW HER...EVERYWHERE SHE'D GO...

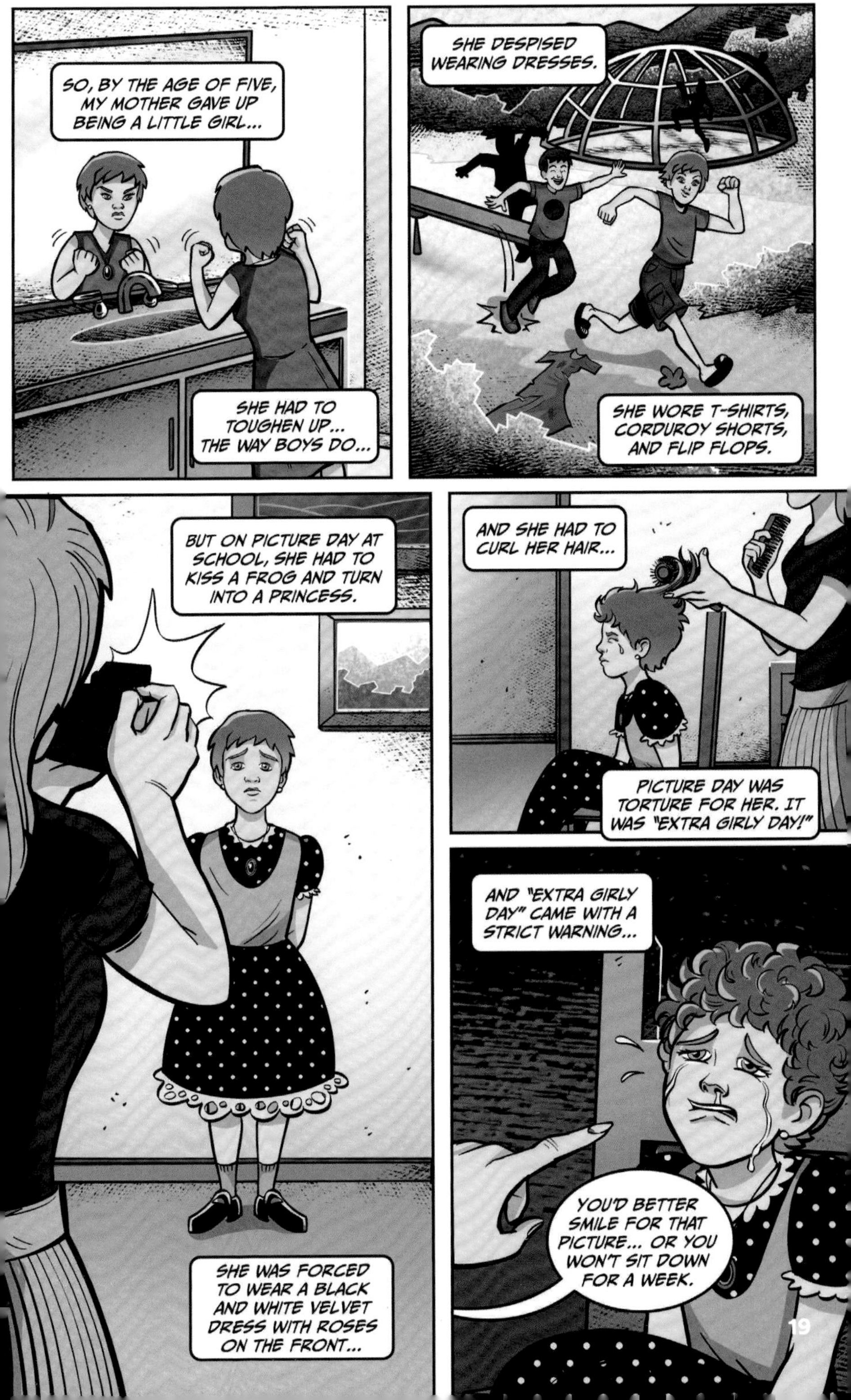

SO, BY THE AGE OF FIVE, MY MOTHER GAVE UP BEING A LITTLE GIRL...
SHE HAD TO TOUGHEN UP... THE WAY BOYS DO...
SHE DESPISED WEARING DRESSES.
SHE WORE T-SHIRTS, CORDUROY SHORTS, AND FLIP FLOPS.
BUT ON PICTURE DAY AT SCHOOL, SHE HAD TO KISS A FROG AND TURN INTO A PRINCESS.
SHE WAS FORCED TO WEAR A BLACK AND WHITE VELVET DRESS WITH ROSES ON THE FRONT...
AND SHE HAD TO CURL HER HAIR...
PICTURE DAY WAS TORTURE FOR HER. IT WAS "EXTRA GIRLY DAY!"
AND "EXTRA GIRLY DAY" CAME WITH A STRICT WARNING...
YOU'D BETTER SMILE FOR THAT PICTURE... OR YOU WON'T SIT DOWN FOR A WEEK.

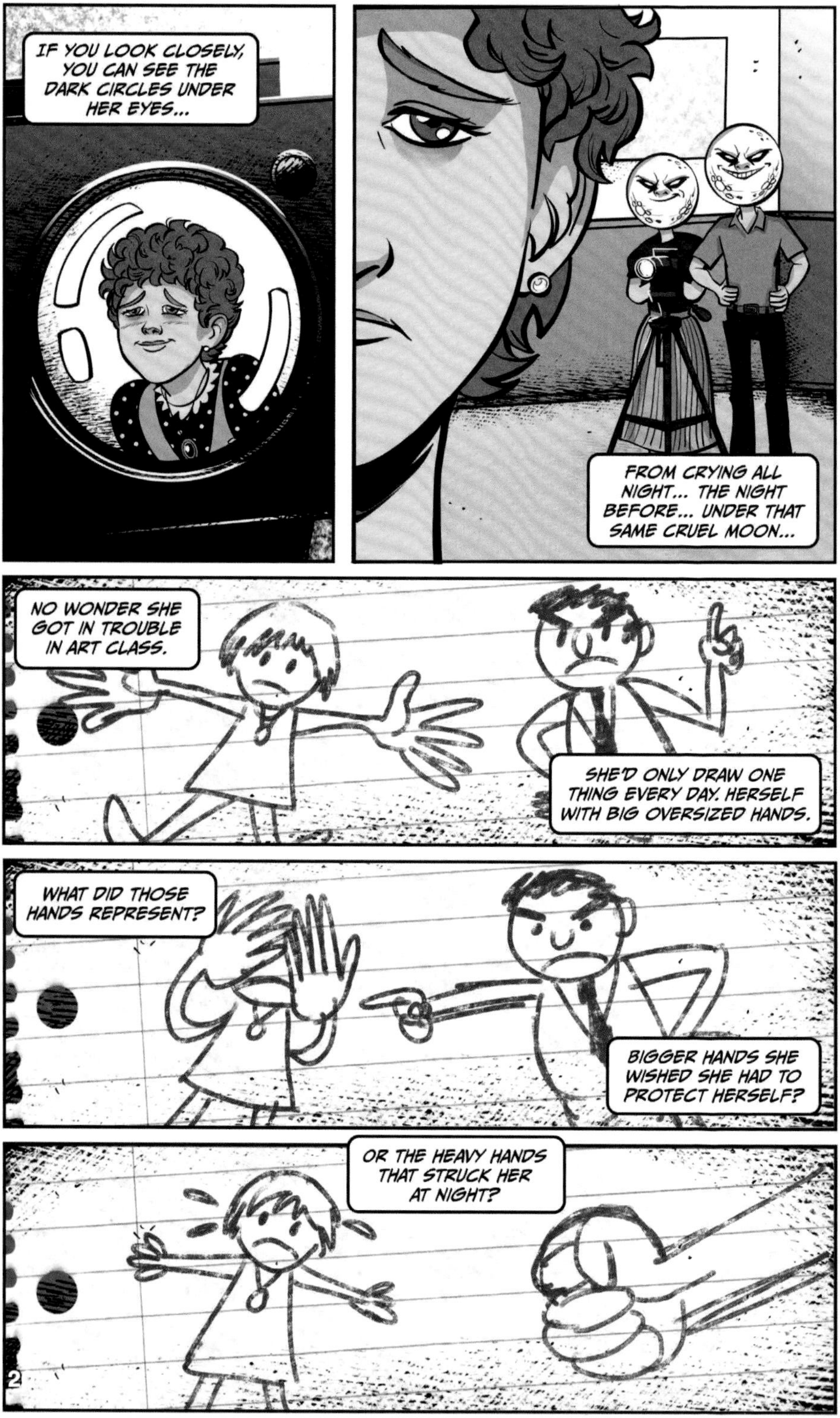
IF YOU LOOK CLOSELY, YOU CAN SEE THE DARK CIRCLES UNDER HER EYES...
FROM CRYING ALL NIGHT... THE NIGHT BEFORE... UNDER THAT SAME CRUEL MOON...
NO WONDER SHE GOT IN TROUBLE IN ART CLASS.
SHE'D ONLY DRAW ONE THING EVERY DAY. HERSELF WITH BIG OVERSIZED HANDS.
WHAT DID THOSE HANDS REPRESENT?
BIGGER HANDS SHE WISHED SHE HAD TO PROTECT HERSELF?
OR THE HEAVY HANDS THAT STRUCK HER AT NIGHT?

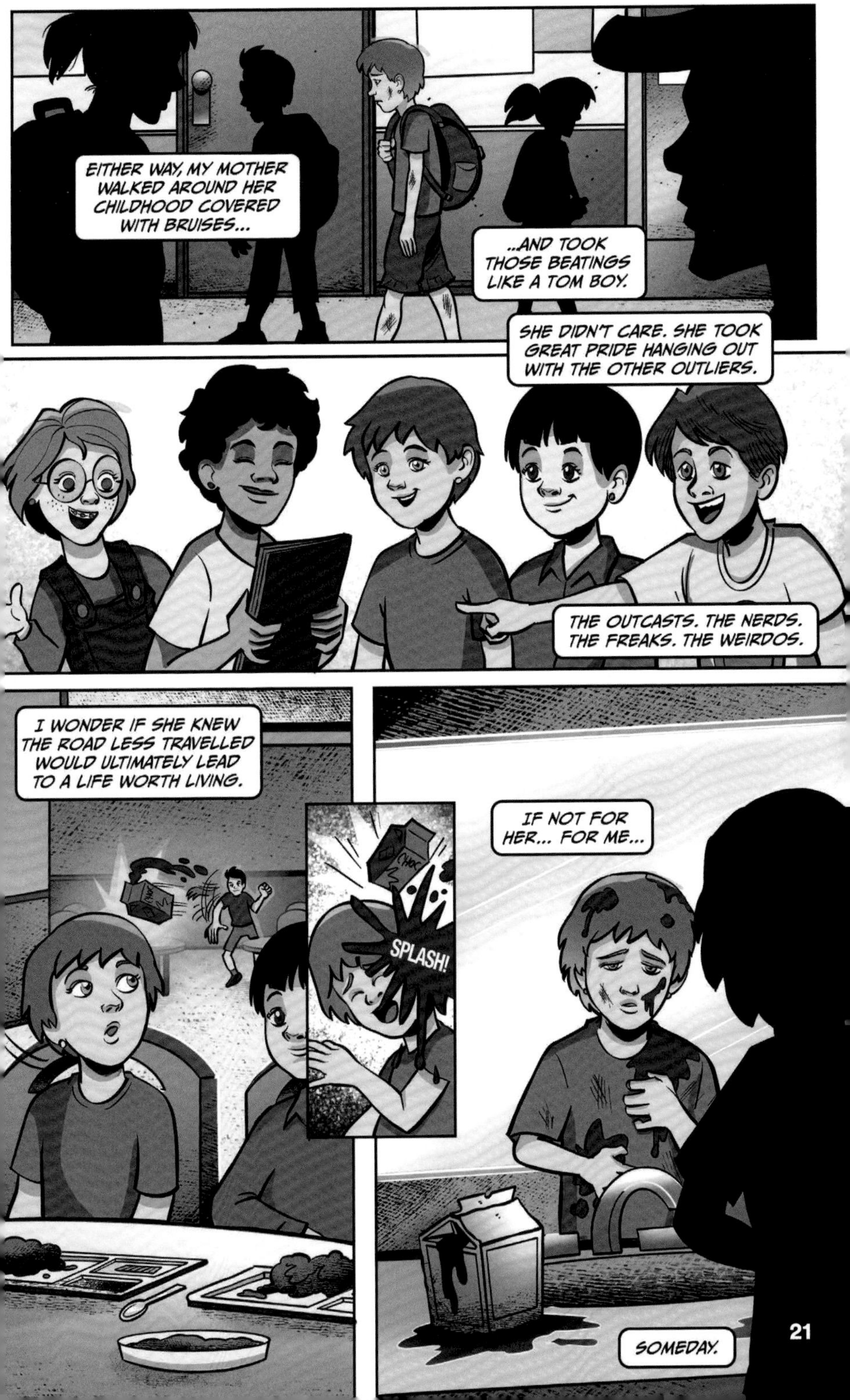
EITHER WAY, MY MOTHER WALKED AROUND HER CHILDHOOD COVERED WITH BRUISES...
...AND TOOK THOSE BEATINGS LIKE A TOM BOY.
SHE DIDN'T CARE. SHE TOOK GREAT PRIDE HANGING OUT WITH THE OTHER OUTLIERS.
THE OUTCASTS. THE NERDS. THE FREAKS. THE WEIRDOS.
I WONDER IF SHE KNEW THE ROAD LESS TRAVELLED WOULD ULTIMATELY LEAD TO A LIFE WORTH LIVING.
SPLASH!
IF NOT FOR HER... FOR ME...
SOMEDAY.

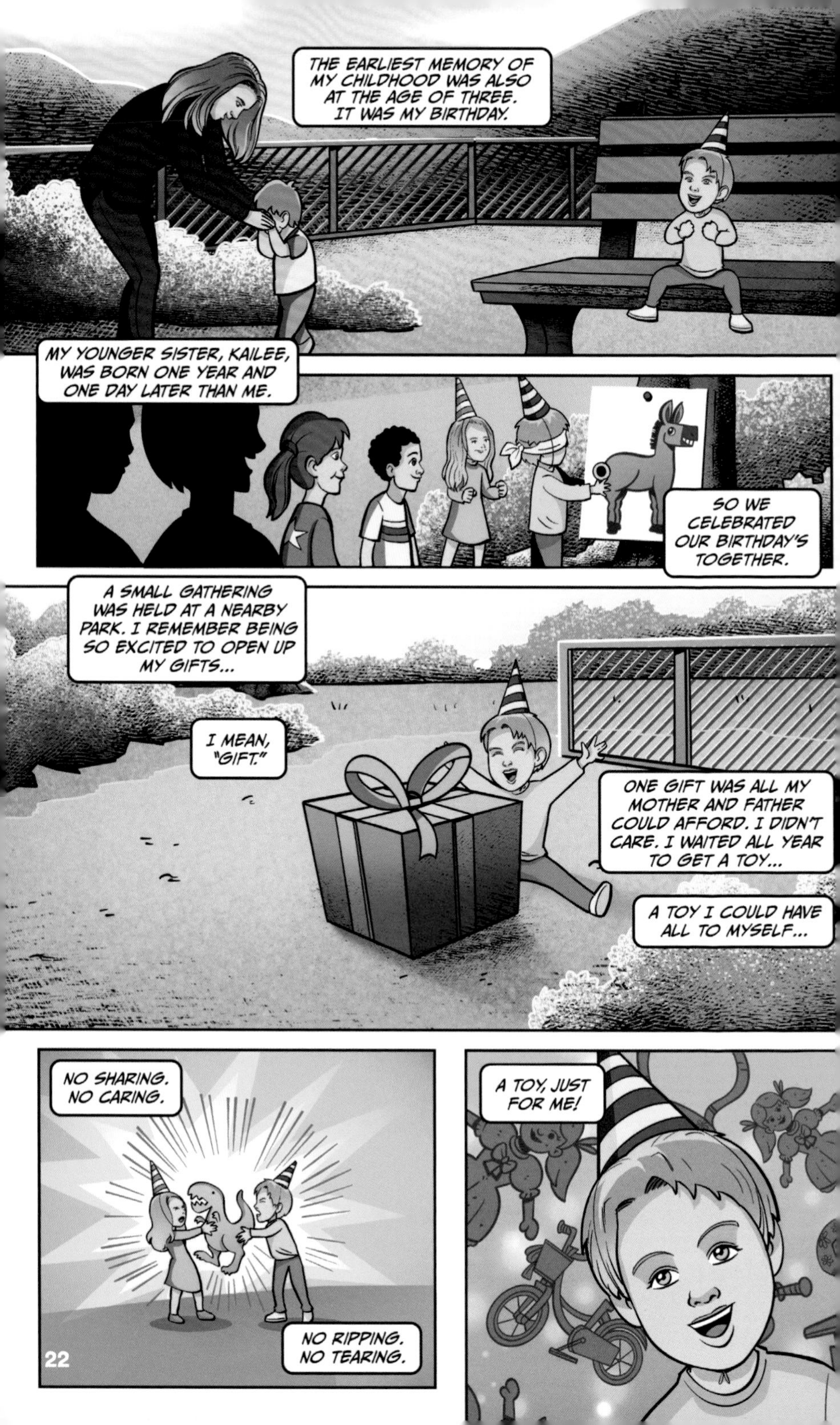
THE EARLIEST MEMORY OF MY CHILDHOOD WAS ALSO AT THE AGE OF THREE. IT WAS MY BIRTHDAY.
MY YOUNGER SISTER, KAILEE, WAS BORN ONE YEAR AND ONE DAY LATER THAN ME.
SO WE CELEBRATED OUR BIRTHDAY'S TOGETHER.
A SMALL GATHERING WAS HELD AT A NEARBY PARK. I REMEMBER BEING SO EXCITED TO OPEN UP MY GIFTS...
I MEAN, "GIFT."
ONE GIFT WAS ALL MY MOTHER AND FATHER COULD AFFORD. I DIDN'T CARE. I WAITED ALL YEAR TO GET A TOY...
A TOY I COULD HAVE ALL TO MYSELF...
NO SHARING. NO CARING.
NO RIPPING. NO TEARING.
A TOY, JUST FOR ME!

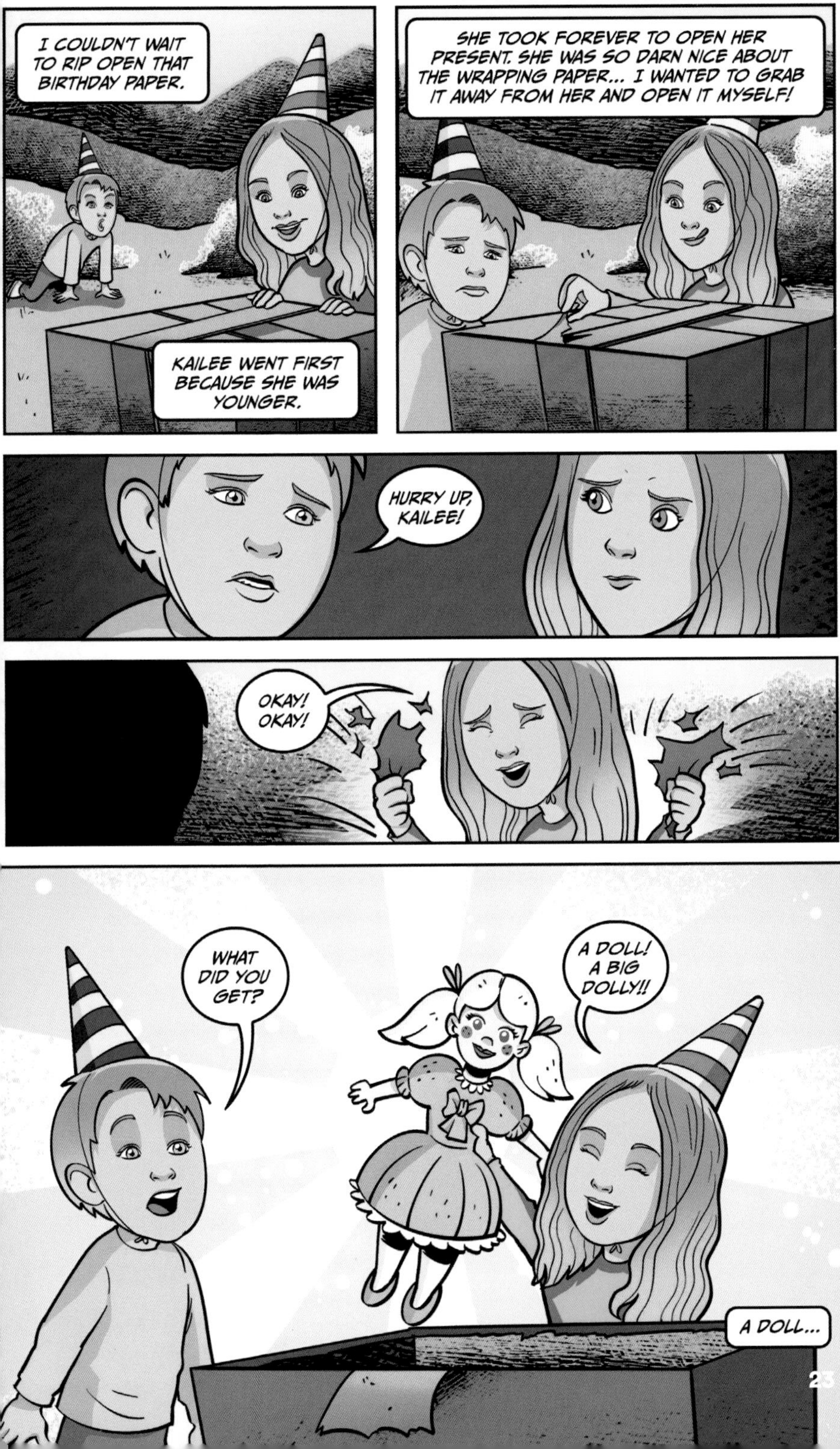

I COULDN'T WAIT TO RIP OPEN THAT BIRTHDAY PAPER.
KAILEE WENT FIRST BECAUSE SHE WAS YOUNGER.
SHE TOOK FOREVER TO OPEN HER PRESENT. SHE WAS SO DARN NICE ABOUT THE WRAPPING PAPER... I WANTED TO GRAB IT AWAY FROM HER AND OPEN IT MYSELF!
HURRY UP, KAILEE!
OKAY! OKAY!
WHAT DID YOU GET?
A DOLL! A BIG DOLLY!!
A DOLL...

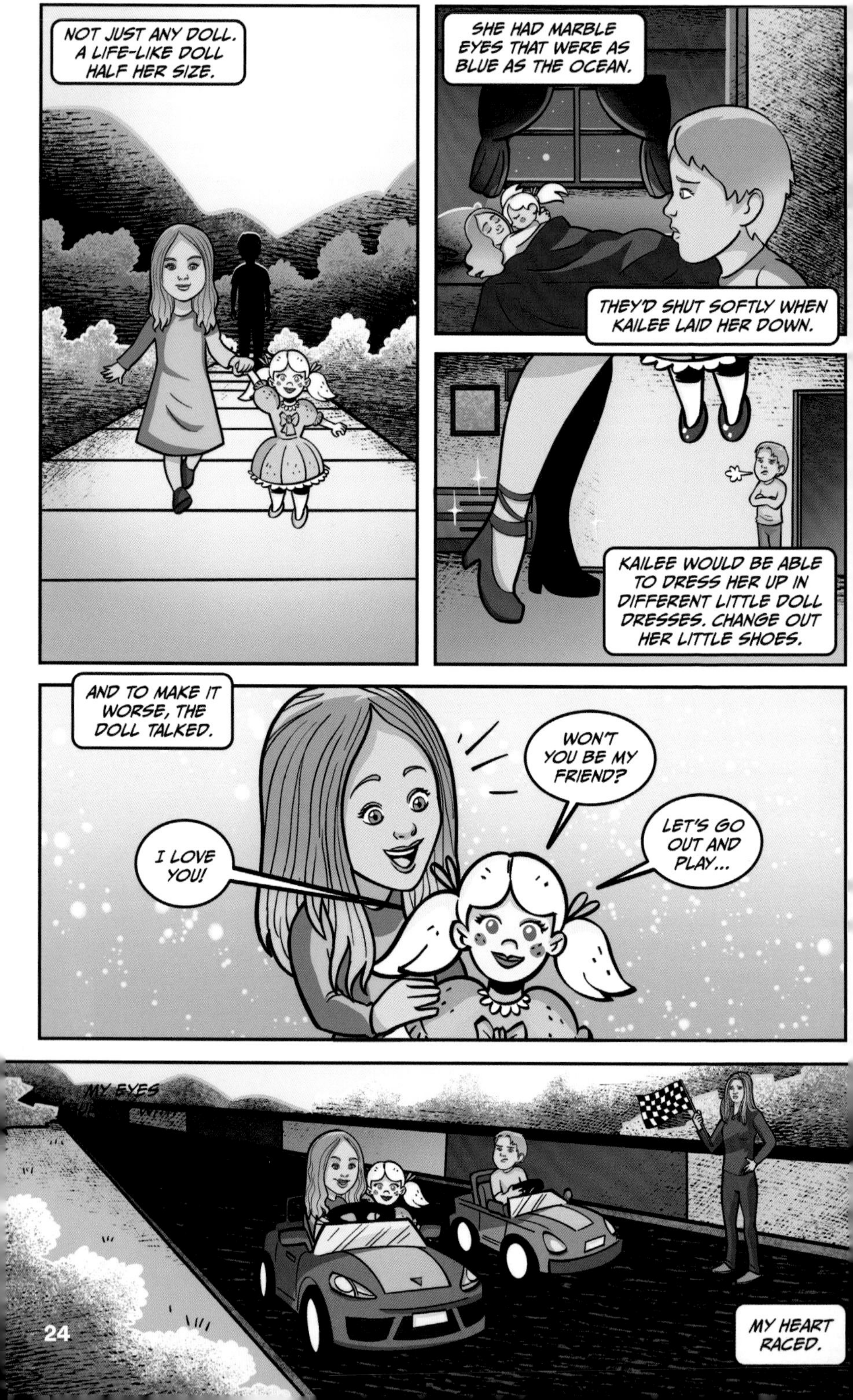
NOT JUST ANY DOLL. A LIFE-LIKE DOLL HALF HER SIZE.
SHE HAD MARBLE EYES THAT WERE AS BLUE AS THE OCEAN.
THEY'D SHUT SOFTLY WHEN KAILEE LAID HER DOWN.
KAILEE WOULD BE ABLE TO DRESS HER UP IN DIFFERENT LITTLE DOLL DRESSES. CHANGE OUT HER LITTLE SHOES.
AND TO MAKE IT WORSE, THE DOLL TALKED.
I LOVE YOU!
WON'T YOU BE MY FRIEND?
LET'S GO OUT AND PLAY...
MY HEART RACED.

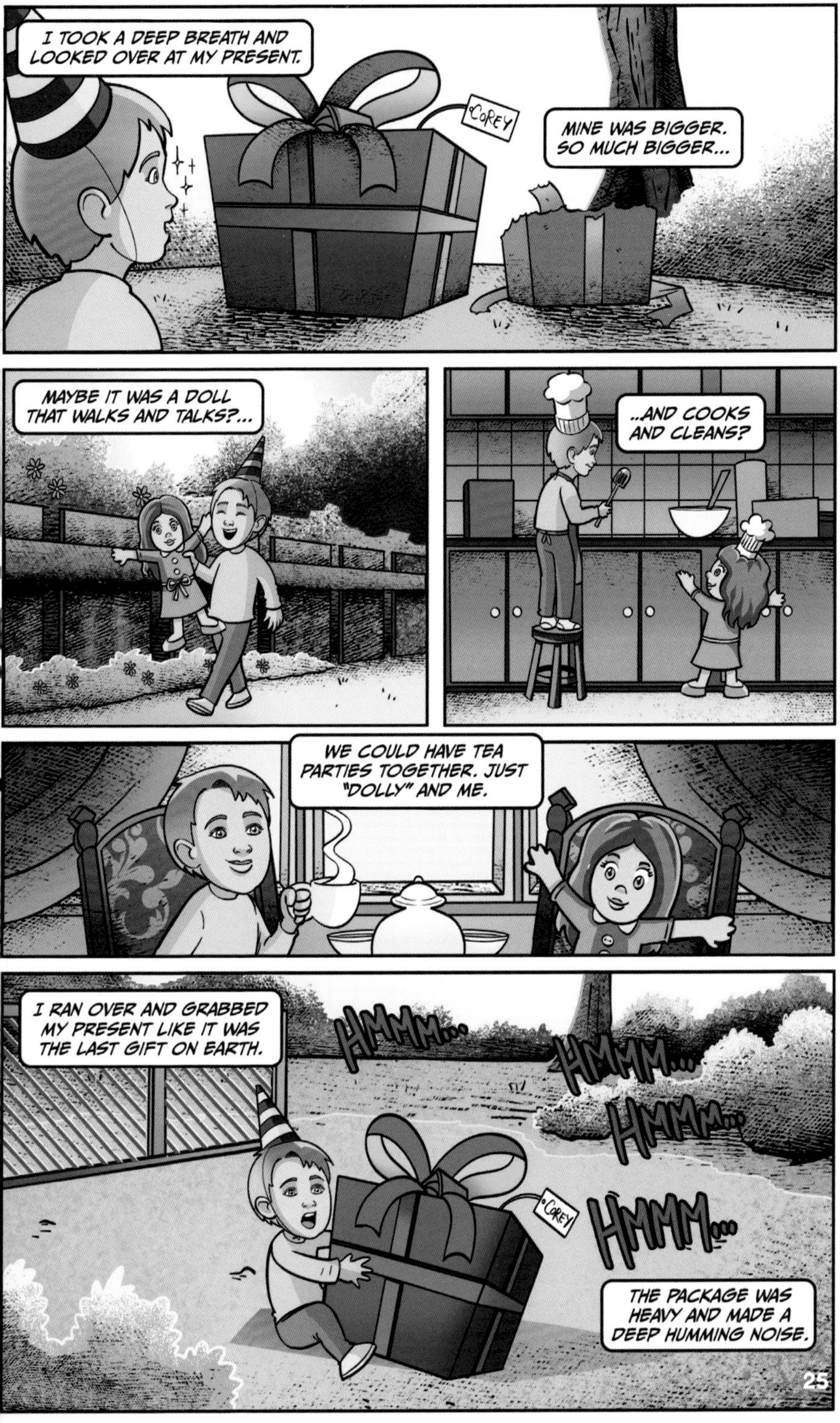

I TOOK A DEEP BREATH AND LOOKED OVER AT MY PRESENT.
COREY
MINE WAS BIGGER. SO MUCH BIGGER...
MAYBE IT WAS A DOLL THAT WALKS AND TALKS?...
..AND COOKS AND CLEANS?
WE COULD HAVE TEA PARTIES TOGETHER. JUST "DOLLY" AND ME.
I RAN OVER AND GRABBED MY PRESENT LIKE IT WAS THE LAST GIFT ON EARTH.
HMMM...
HMMM...
HMMM...
COREY
HMMM...
THE PACKAGE WAS HEAVY AND MADE A DEEP HUMMING NOISE.

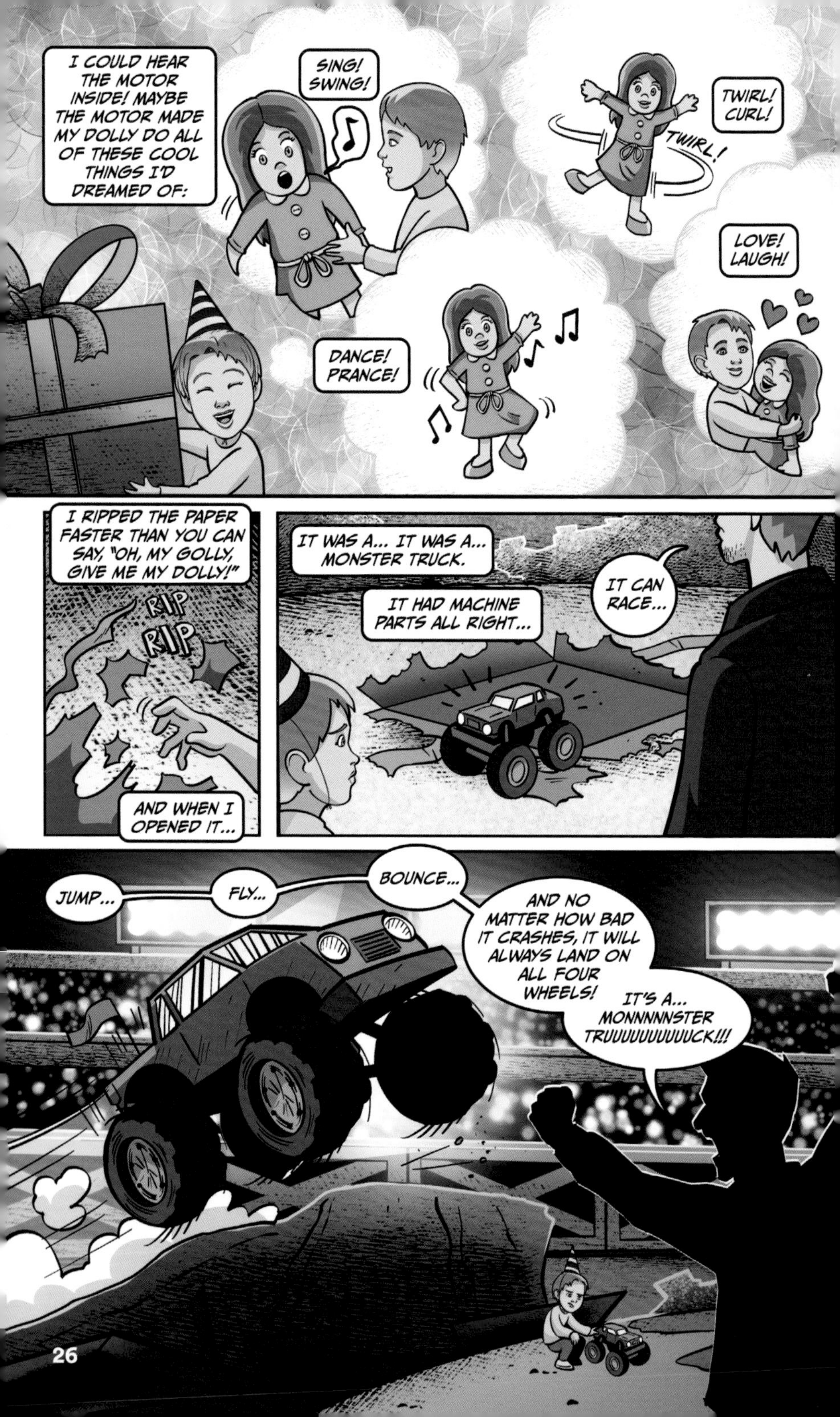
I COULD HEAR THE MOTOR INSIDE! MAYBE THE MOTOR MADE MY DOLLY DO ALL OF THESE COOL THINGS I'D DREAMED OF:
SING! SWING!
TWIRL! CURL!
TWIRL!
DANCE! PRANCE!
LOVE! LAUGH!
I RIPPED THE PAPER FASTER THAN YOU CAN SAY, "OH, MY GOLLY, GIVE ME MY DOLLY!"
RIP
RIP
AND WHEN I OPENED IT...
IT WAS A... IT WAS A... MONSTER TRUCK.
IT HAD MACHINE PARTS ALL RIGHT...
IT CAN RACE...
JUMP...
FLY...
BOUNCE...
AND NO MATTER HOW BAD IT CRASHES, IT WILL ALWAYS LAND ON ALL FOUR WHEELS!
IT'S A... MONNNNNSTER TRUUUUUUUUUUCK!!!

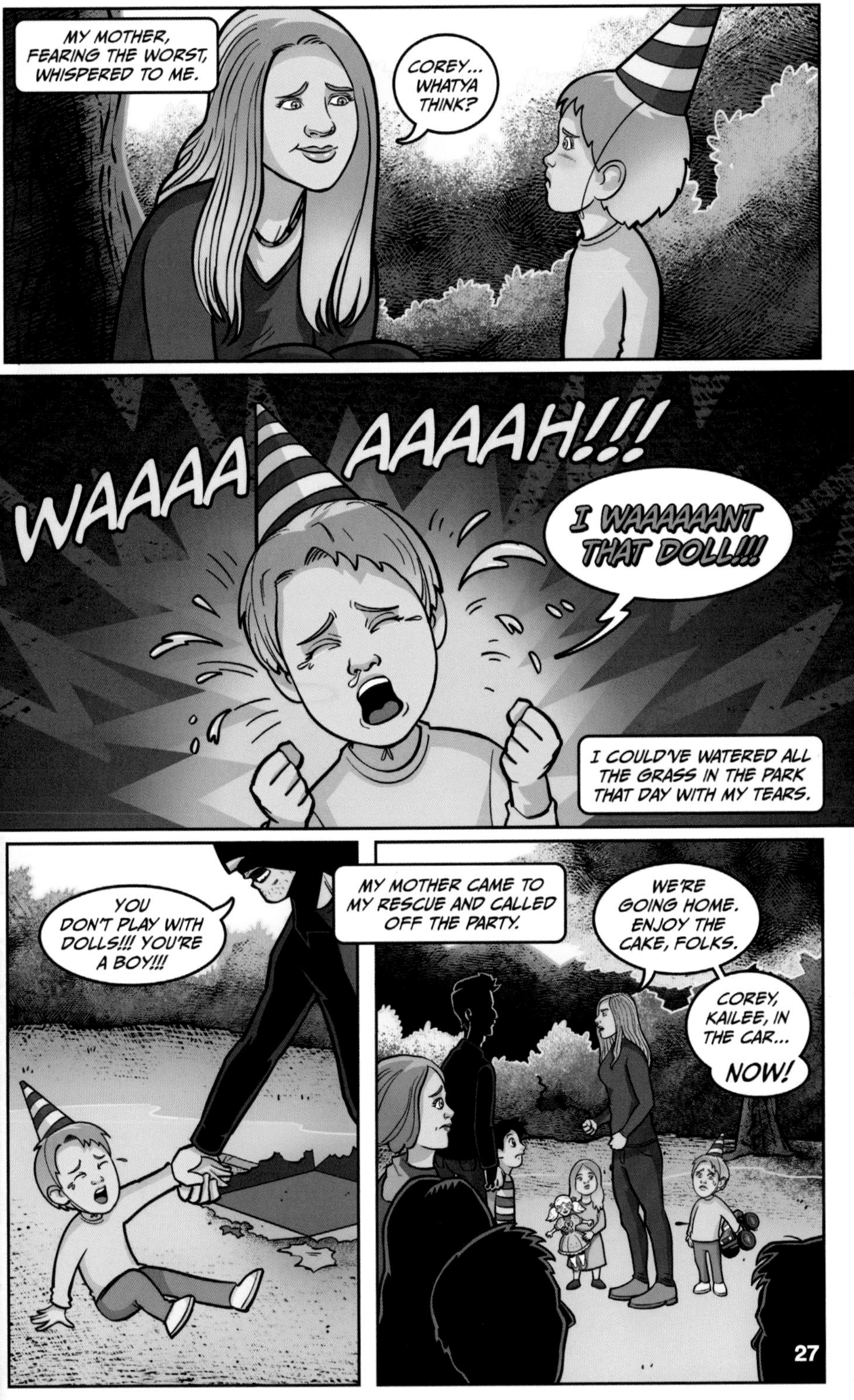
MY MOTHER, FEARING THE WORST, WHISPERED TO ME.
COREY... WHATYA THINK?
WAAAA AAAAH!!!
I WAAAAAANT THAT DOLL!!!
I COULD'VE WATERED ALL THE GRASS IN THE PARK THAT DAY WITH MY TEARS.
YOU DON'T PLAY WITH DOLLS!!! YOU'RE A BOY!!!
MY MOTHER CAME TO MY RESCUE AND CALLED OFF THE PARTY.
WE'RE GOING HOME. ENJOY THE CAKE, FOLKS.
COREY, KAILEE, IN THE CAR... NOW!

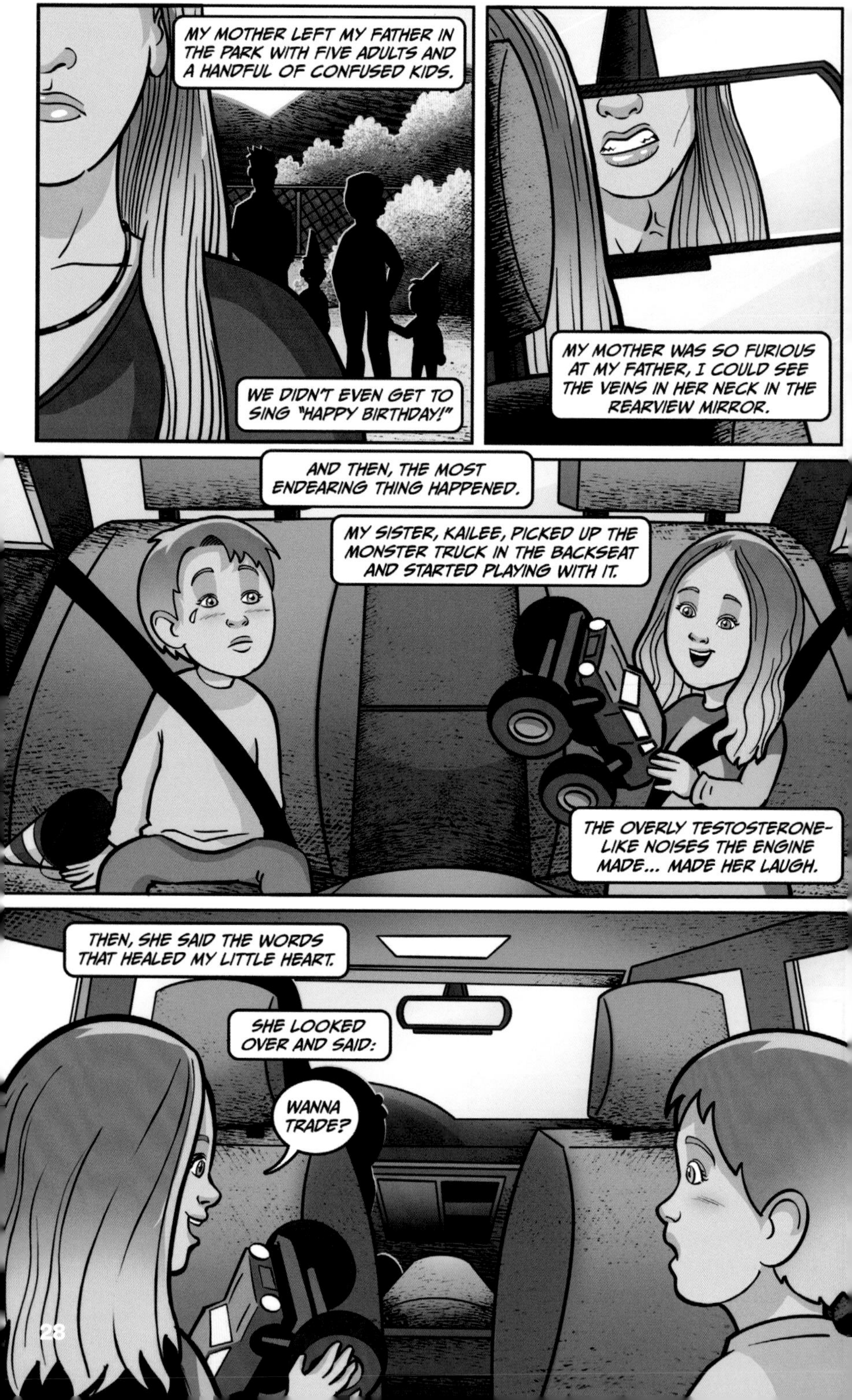
MY MOTHER LEFT MY FATHER IN THE PARK WITH FIVE ADULTS AND A HANDFUL OF CONFUSED KIDS.
WE DIDN'T EVEN GET TO SING "HAPPY BIRTHDAY!"
MY MOTHER WAS SO FURIOUS AT MY FATHER, I COULD SEE THE VEINS IN HER NECK IN THE REARVIEW MIRROR.
AND THEN, THE MOST ENDEARING THING HAPPENED.
MY SISTER, KAILEE, PICKED UP THE MONSTER TRUCK IN THE BACKSEAT AND STARTED PLAYING WITH IT.
THE OVERLY TESTOSTERONE-LIKE NOISES THE ENGINE MADE... MADE HER LAUGH.
THEN, SHE SAID THE WORDS THAT HEALED MY LITTLE HEART.
SHE LOOKED OVER AND SAID:
WANNA TRADE?

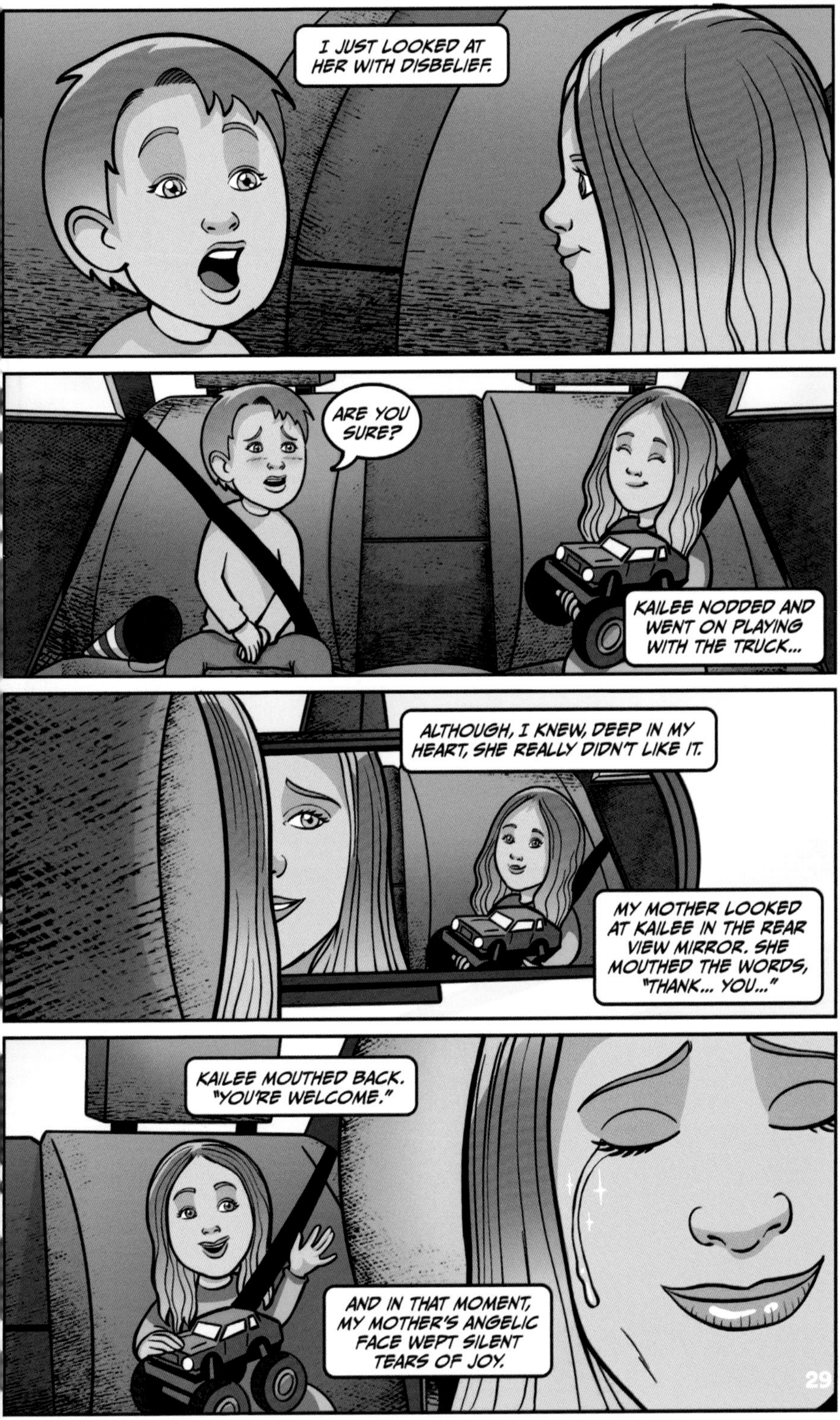
I JUST LOOKED AT HER WITH DISBELIEF.
ARE YOU SURE?
KAILEE NODDED AND WENT ON PLAYING WITH THE TRUCK...
ALTHOUGH, I KNEW, DEEP IN MY HEART, SHE REALLY DIDN'T LIKE IT.
MY MOTHER LOOKED AT KAILEE IN THE REAR VIEW MIRROR. SHE MOUTHED THE WORDS, "THANK... YOU..."
KAILEE MOUTHED BACK. "YOU'RE WELCOME."
AND IN THAT MOMENT, MY MOTHER'S ANGELIC FACE WEPT SILENT TEARS OF JOY.

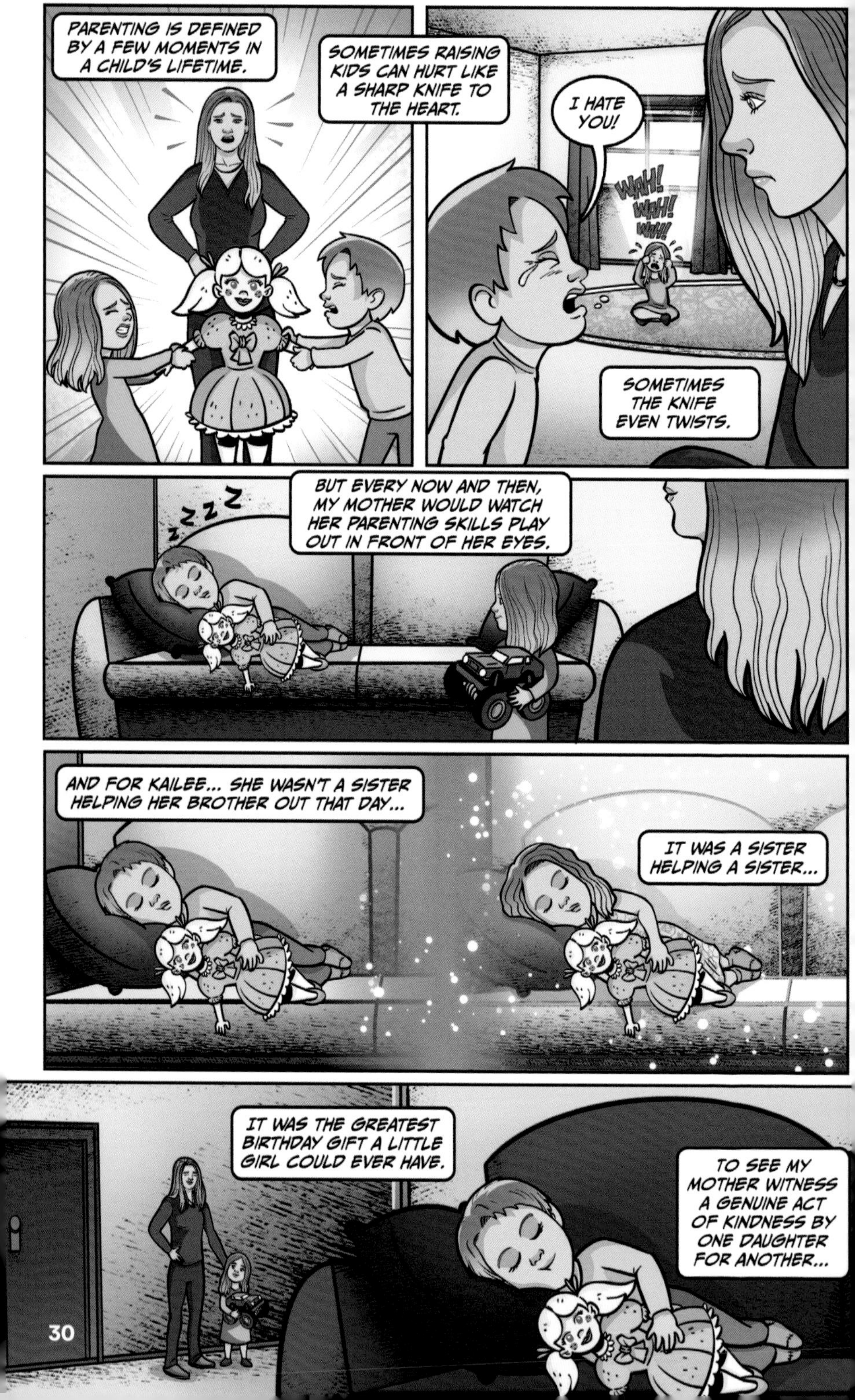
PARENTING IS DEFINED BY A FEW MOMENTS IN A CHILD'S LIFETIME.
SOMETIMES RAISING KIDS CAN HURT LIKE A SHARP KNIFE TO THE HEART.
I HATE YOU!
WAH! WAH! WAH!
SOMETIMES THE KNIFE EVEN TWISTS.
Z Z Z Z
BUT EVERY NOW AND THEN, MY MOTHER WOULD WATCH HER PARENTING SKILLS PLAY OUT IN FRONT OF HER EYES.
AND FOR KAILEE... SHE WASN'T A SISTER HELPING HER BROTHER OUT THAT DAY...
IT WAS A SISTER HELPING A SISTER...
IT WAS THE GREATEST BIRTHDAY GIFT A LITTLE GIRL COULD EVER HAVE.
TO SEE MY MOTHER WITNESS A GENUINE ACT OF KINDNESS BY ONE DAUGHTER FOR ANOTHER...

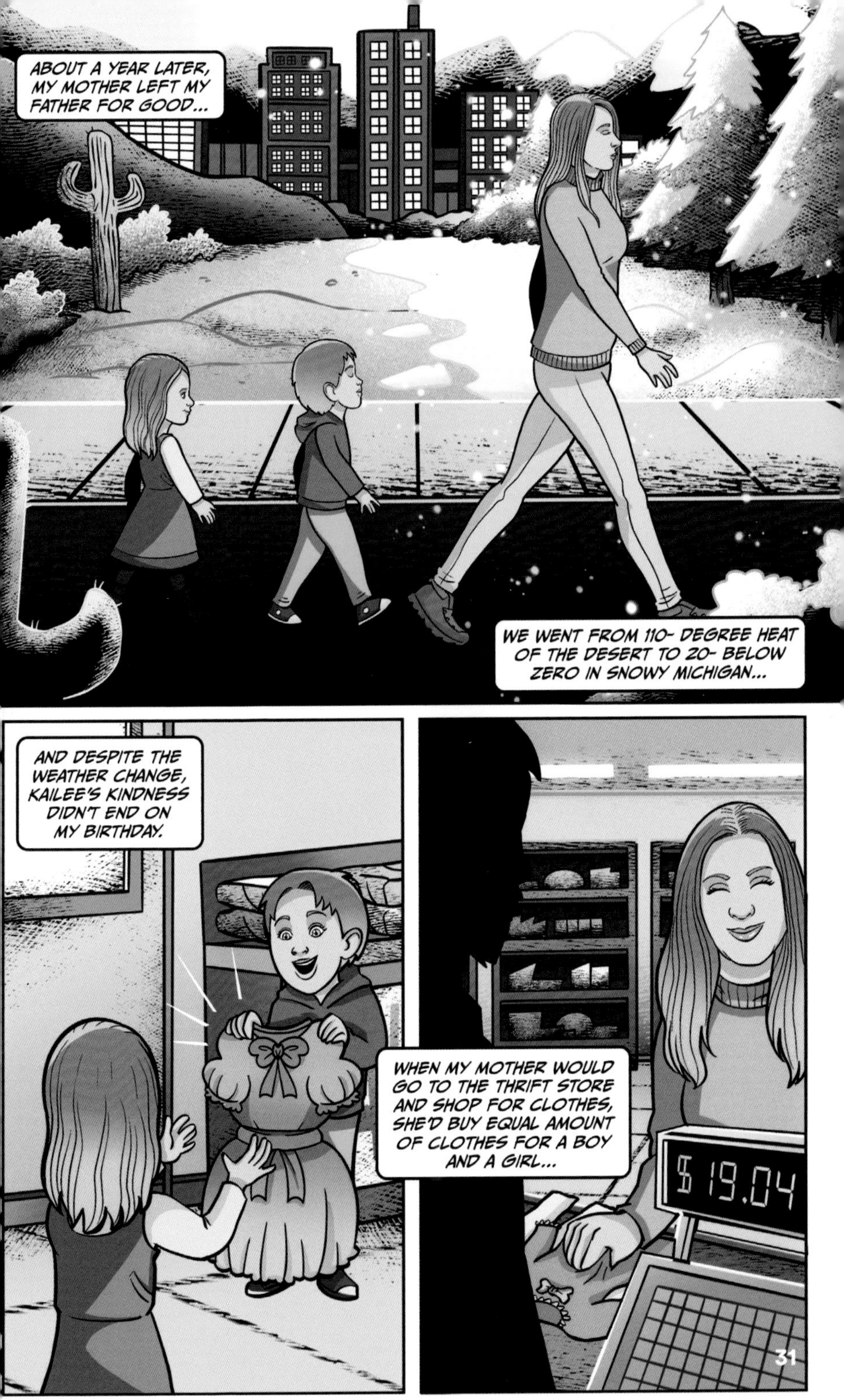
ABOUT A YEAR LATER, MY MOTHER LEFT MY FATHER FOR GOOD...
WE WENT FROM 110- DEGREE HEAT OF THE DESERT TO 20- BELOW ZERO IN SNOWY MICHIGAN...
AND DESPITE THE WEATHER CHANGE, KAILEE'S KINDNESS DIDN'T END ON MY BIRTHDAY.
WHEN MY MOTHER WOULD GO TO THE THRIFT STORE AND SHOP FOR CLOTHES, SHE'D BUY EQUAL AMOUNT OF CLOTHES FOR A BOY AND A GIRL...
$ 19.04

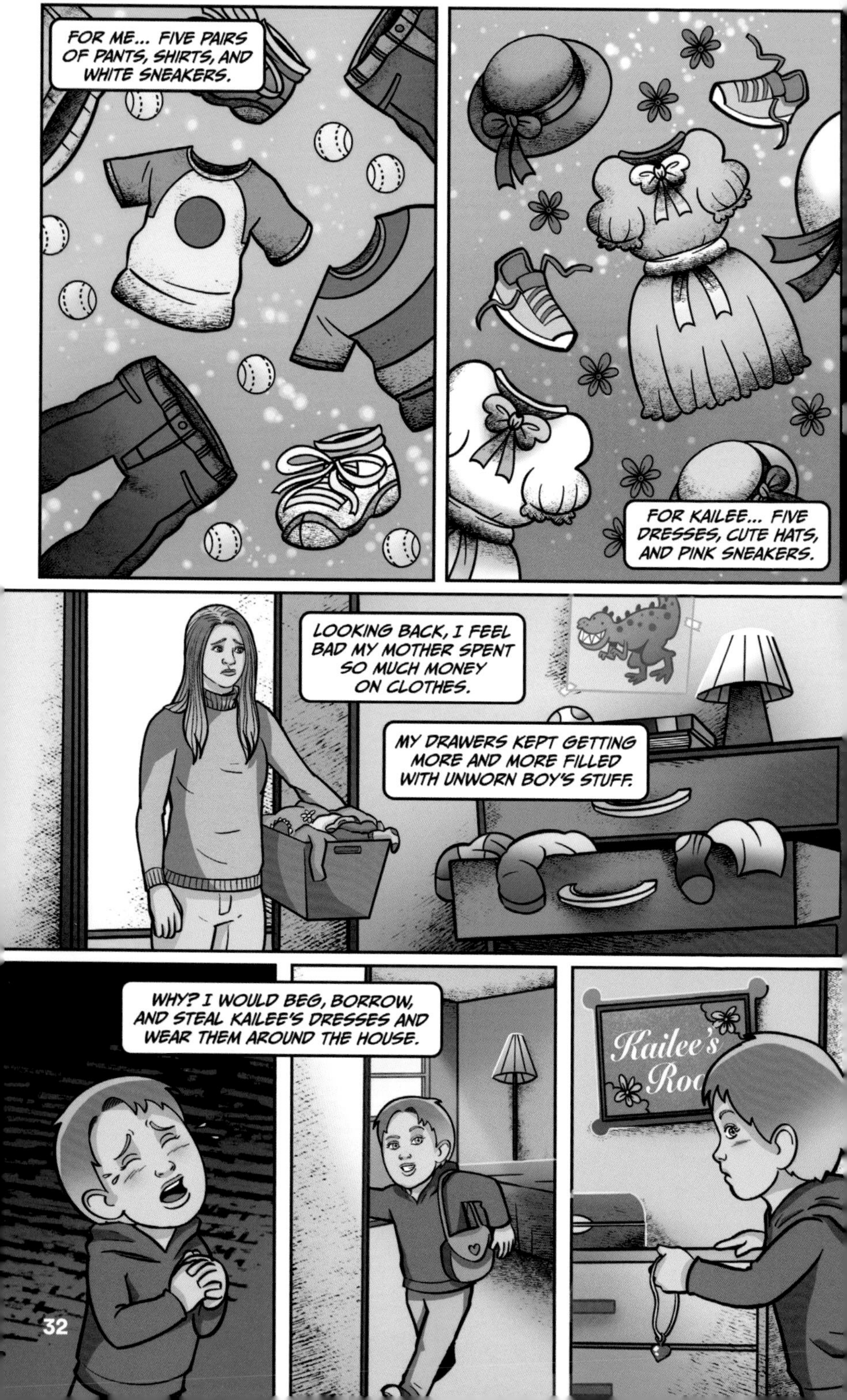
FOR ME... FIVE PAIRS OF PANTS, SHIRTS, AND WHITE SNEAKERS.
FOR KAILEE... FIVE DRESSES, CUTE HATS, AND PINK SNEAKERS.
LOOKING BACK, I FEEL BAD MY MOTHER SPENT SO MUCH MONEY ON CLOTHES.
MY DRAWERS KEPT GETTING MORE AND MORE FILLED WITH UNWORN BOY'S STUFF.
WHY? I WOULD BEG, BORROW, AND STEAL KAILEE'S DRESSES AND WEAR THEM AROUND THE HOUSE.

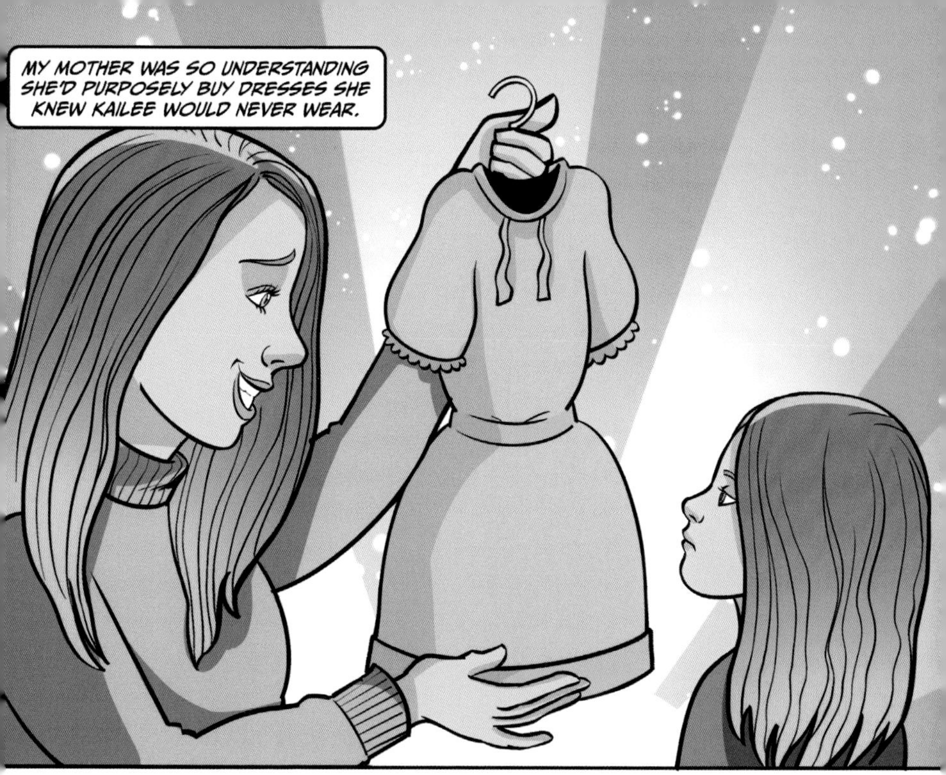
MY MOTHER WAS SO UNDERSTANDING SHE'D PURPOSELY BUY DRESSES SHE KNEW KAILEE WOULD NEVER WEAR.

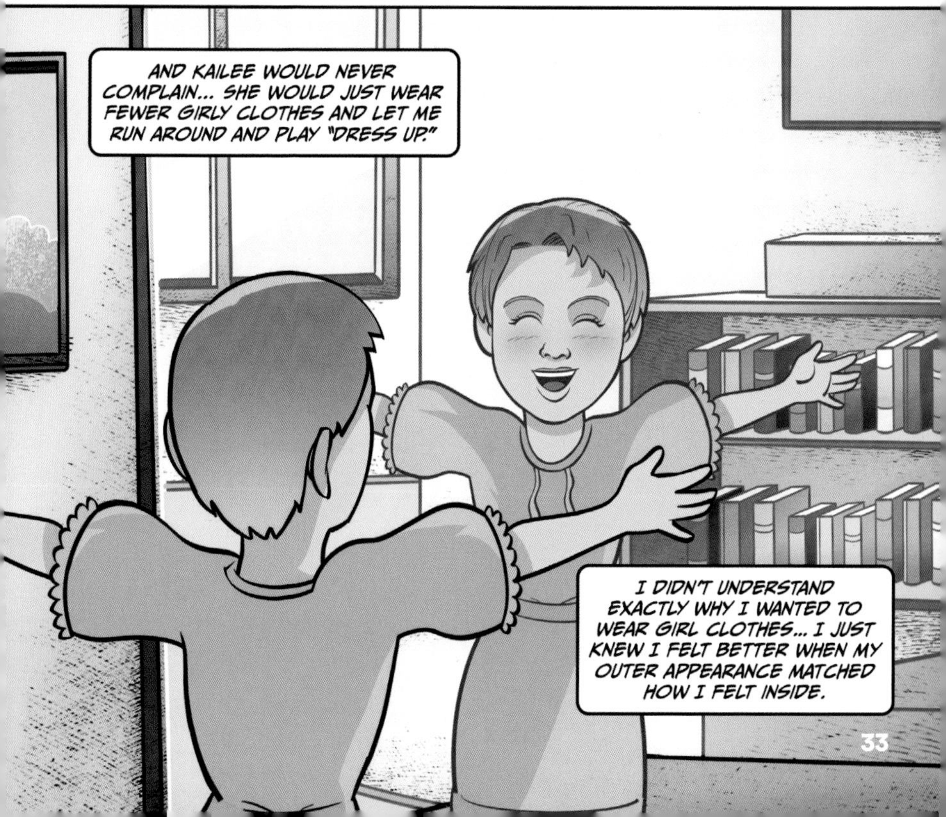
AND KAILEE WOULD NEVER COMPLAIN... SHE WOULD JUST WEAR FEWER GIRLY CLOTHES AND LET ME RUN AROUND AND PLAY "DRESS UP."
I DIDN'T UNDERSTAND EXACTLY WHY I WANTED TO WEAR GIRL CLOTHES... I JUST KNEW I FELT BETTER WHEN MY OUTER APPEARANCE MATCHED HOW I FELT INSIDE.

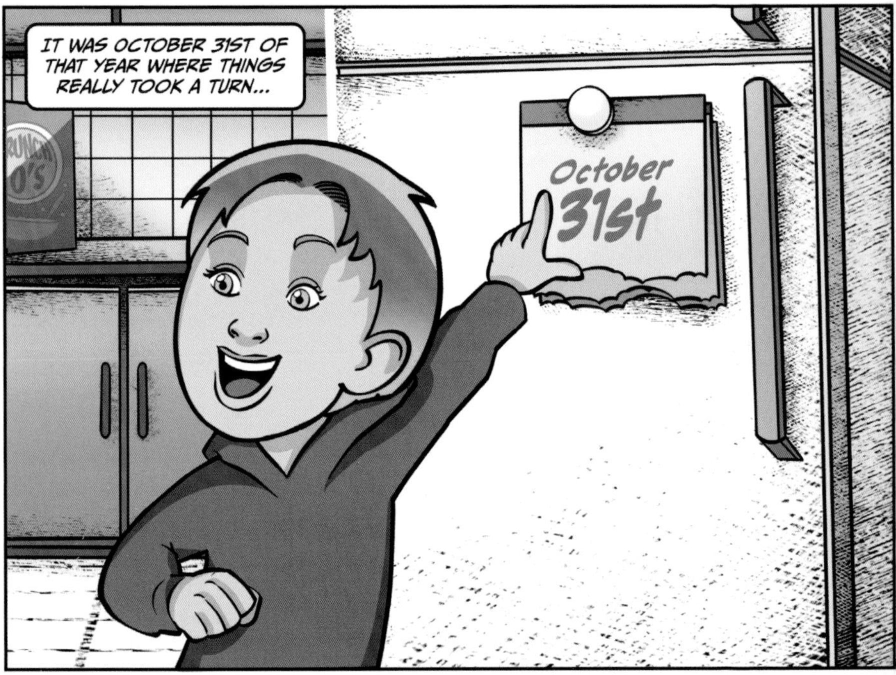
IT WAS OCTOBER 31ST OF THAT YEAR WHERE THINGS REALLY TOOK A TURN...
October 31st

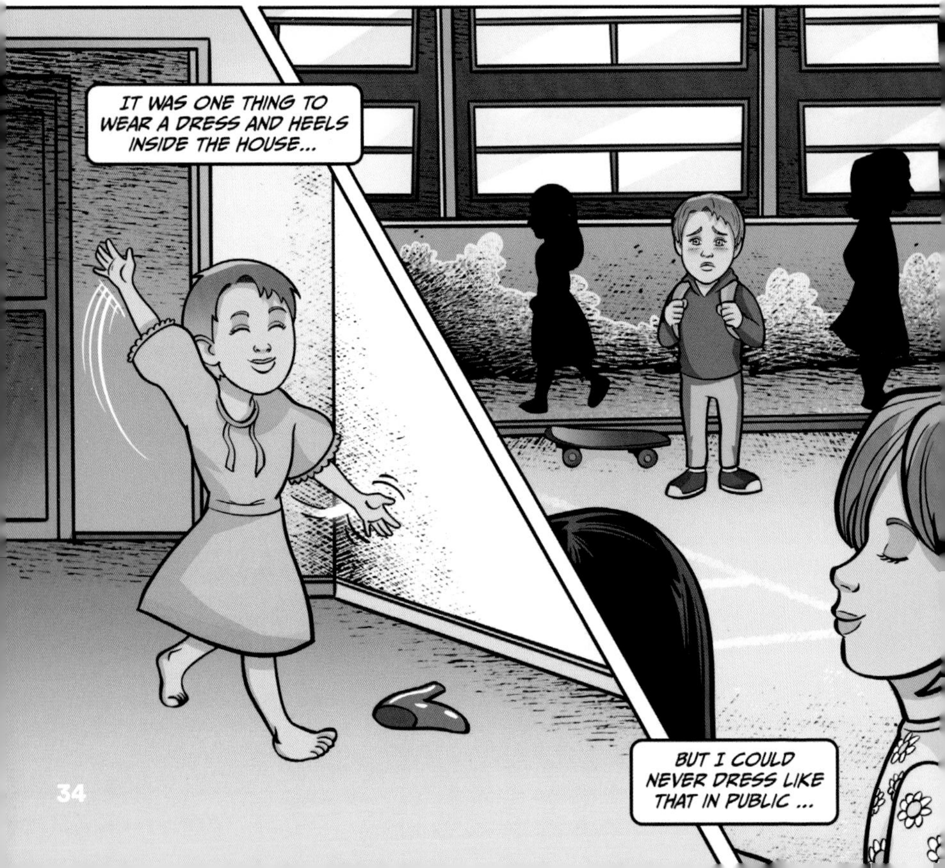
IT WAS ONE THING TO WEAR A DRESS AND HEELS INSIDE THE HOUSE...
BUT I COULD NEVER DRESS LIKE THAT IN PUBLIC ...

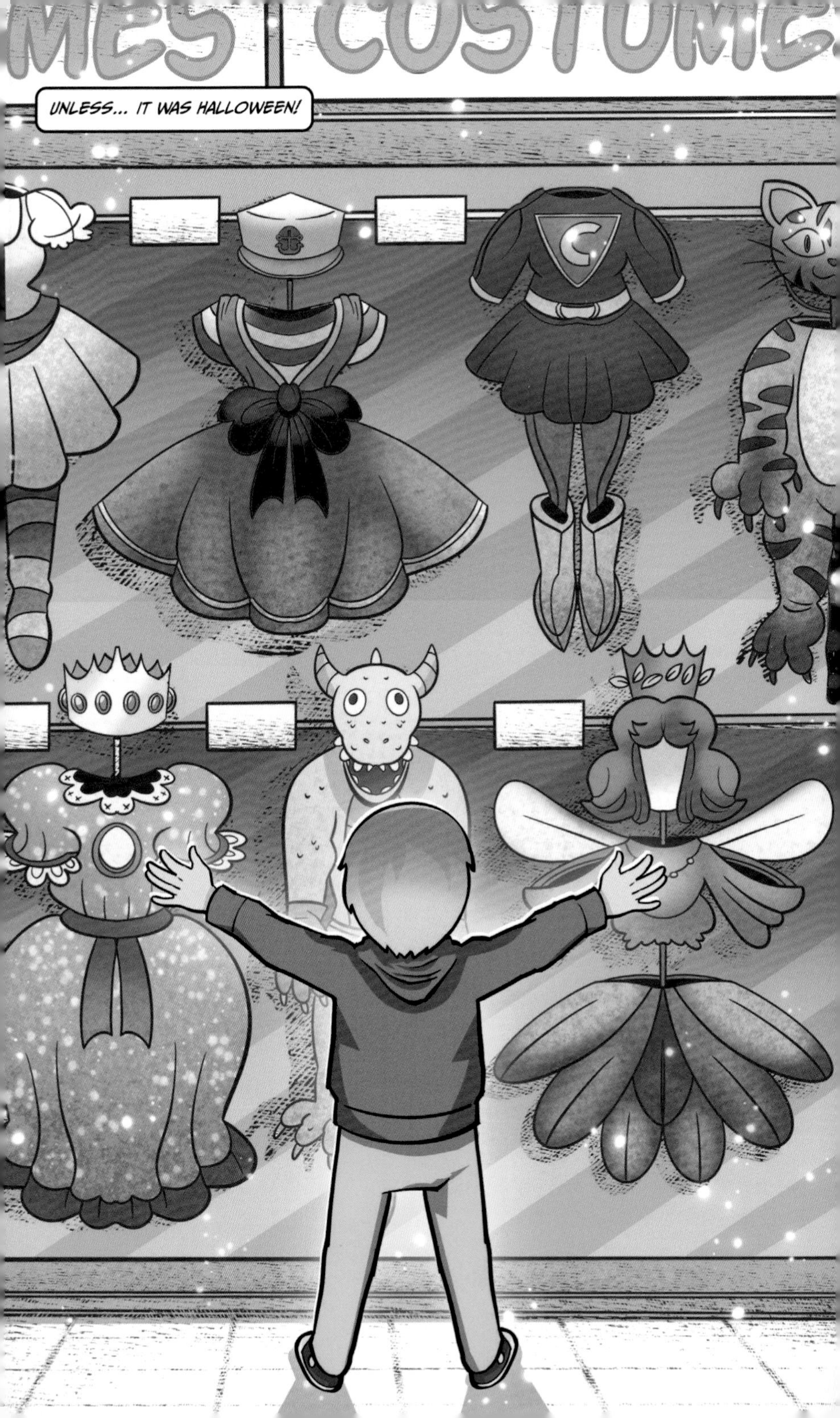
MES
COSTUME
UNLESS... IT WAS HALLOWEEN!

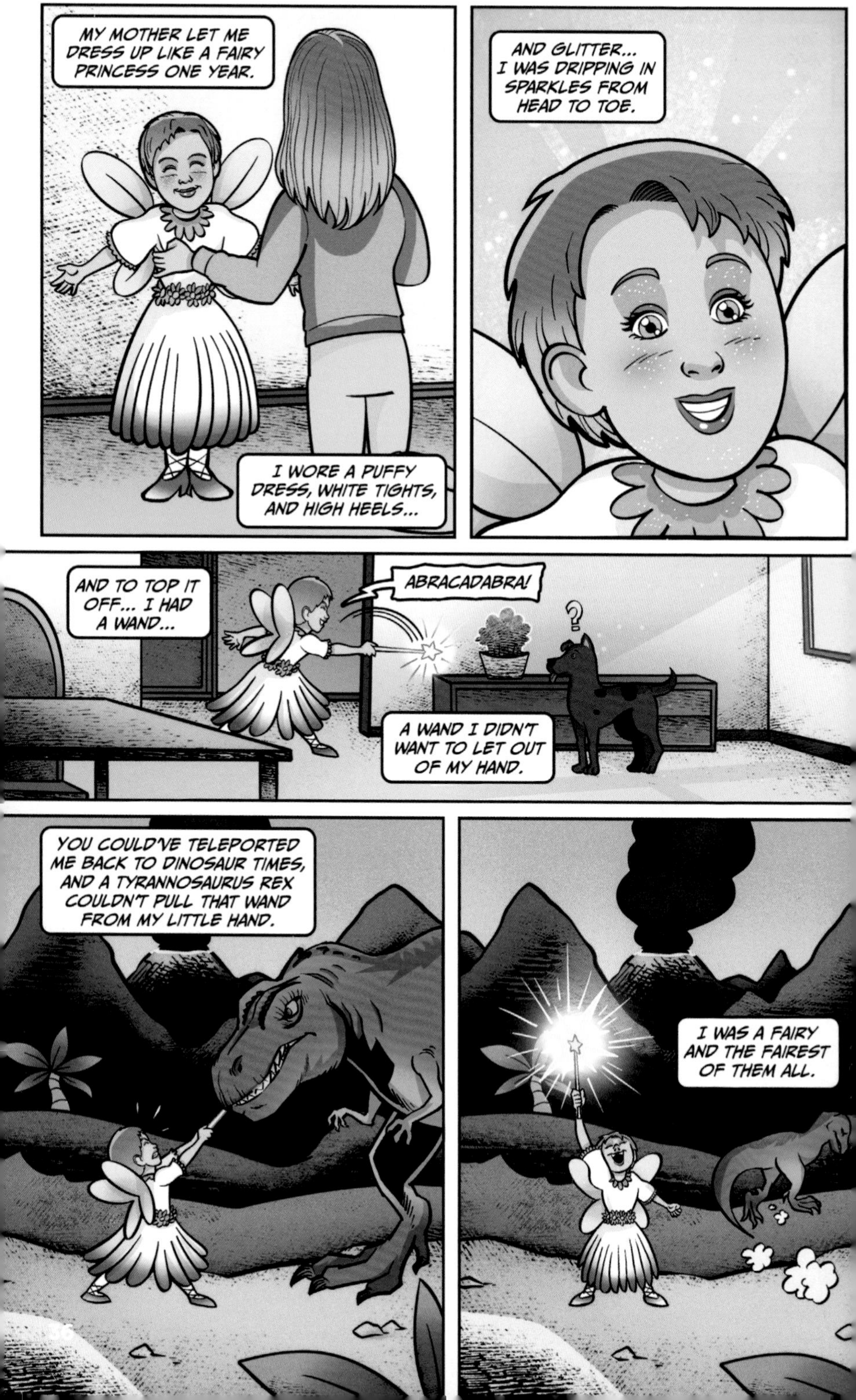
MY MOTHER LET ME DRESS UP LIKE A FAIRY PRINCESS ONE YEAR.
I WORE A PUFFY DRESS, WHITE TIGHTS, AND HIGH HEELS...
AND GLITTER... I WAS DRIPPING IN SPARKLES FROM HEAD TO TOE.
AND TO TOP IT OFF... I HAD A WAND...
ABRACADABRA!
?
A WAND I DIDN'T WANT TO LET OUT OF MY HAND.
YOU COULD'VE TELEPORTED ME BACK TO DINOSAUR TIMES, AND A TYRANNOSAURUS REX COULDN'T PULL THAT WAND FROM MY LITTLE HAND.
I WAS A FAIRY AND THE FAIREST OF THEM ALL.

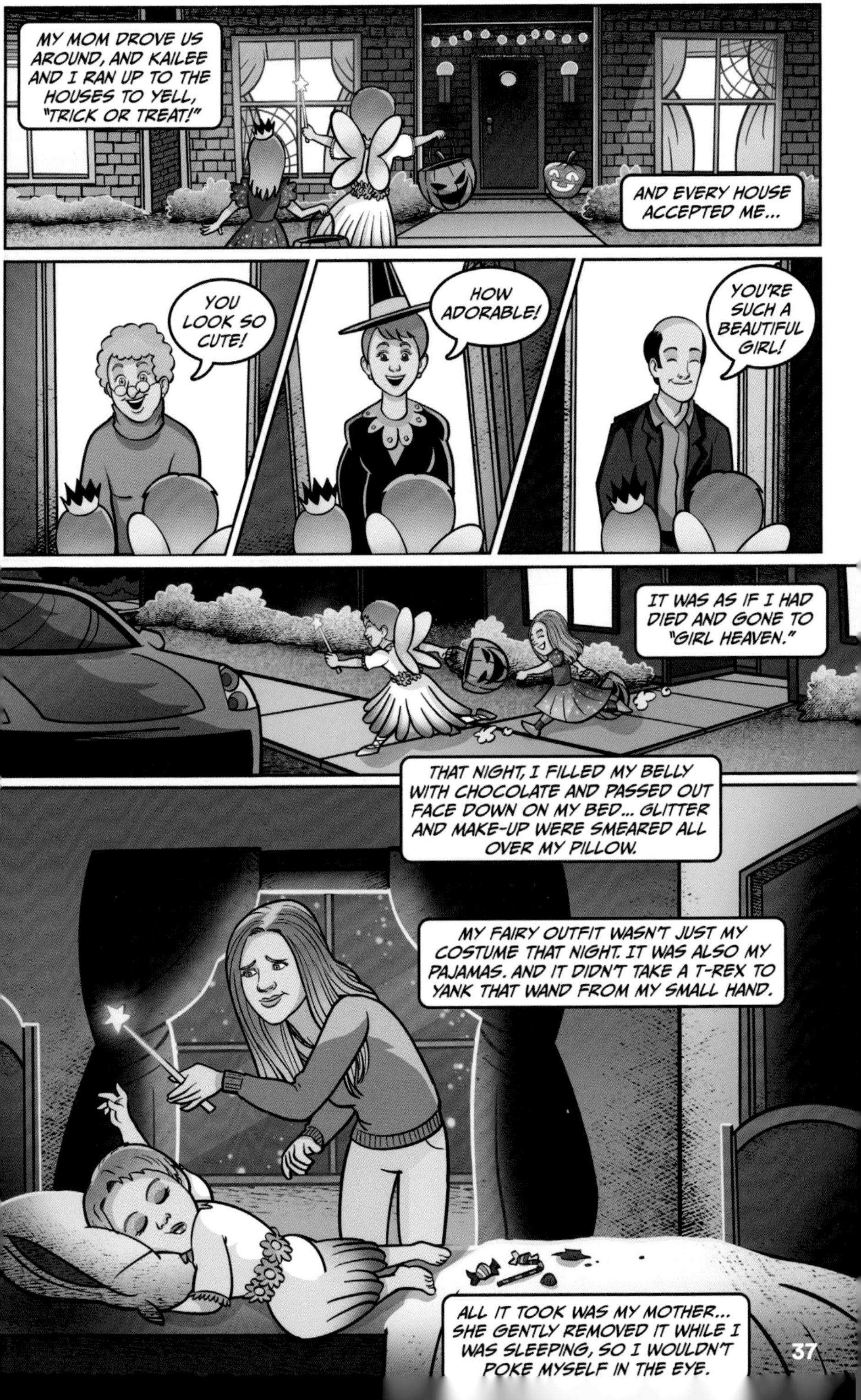
MY MOM DROVE US AROUND, AND KAILEE AND I RAN UP TO THE HOUSES TO YELL, "TRICK OR TREAT!"
AND EVERY HOUSE ACCEPTED ME...
YOU LOOK SO CUTE!
HOW ADORABLE!
YOU'RE SUCH A BEAUTIFUL GIRL!
IT WAS AS IF I HAD DIED AND GONE TO "GIRL HEAVEN."
THAT NIGHT, I FILLED MY BELLY WITH CHOCOLATE AND PASSED OUT FACE DOWN ON MY BED... GLITTER AND MAKE-UP WERE SMEARED ALL OVER MY PILLOW.
MY FAIRY OUTFIT WASN'T JUST MY COSTUME THAT NIGHT. IT WAS ALSO MY PAJAMAS. AND IT DIDN'T TAKE A T-REX TO YANK THAT WAND FROM MY SMALL HAND.
ALL IT TOOK WAS MY MOTHER... SHE GENTLY REMOVED IT WHILE I WAS SLEEPING, SO I WOULDN'T POKE MYSELF IN THE EYE.

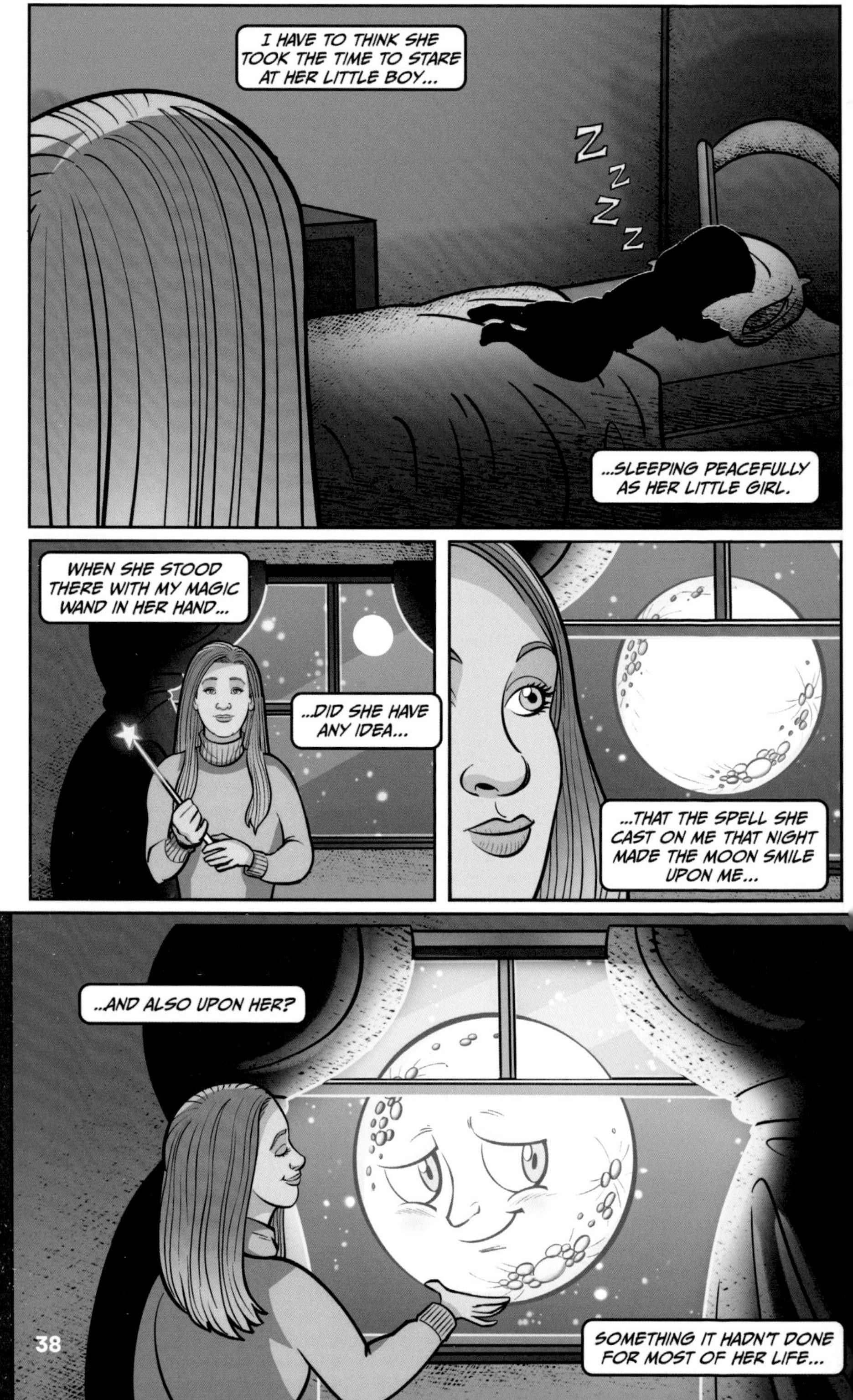
I HAVE TO THINK SHE TOOK THE TIME TO STARE AT HER LITTLE BOY...
Z Z Z Z
...SLEEPING PEACEFULLY AS HER LITTLE GIRL.
WHEN SHE STOOD THERE WITH MY MAGIC WAND IN HER HAND...
...DID SHE HAVE ANY IDEA...
...THAT THE SPELL SHE CAST ON ME THAT NIGHT MADE THE MOON SMILE UPON ME...
...AND ALSO UPON HER?
SOMETHING IT HADN'T DONE FOR MOST OF HER LIFE...

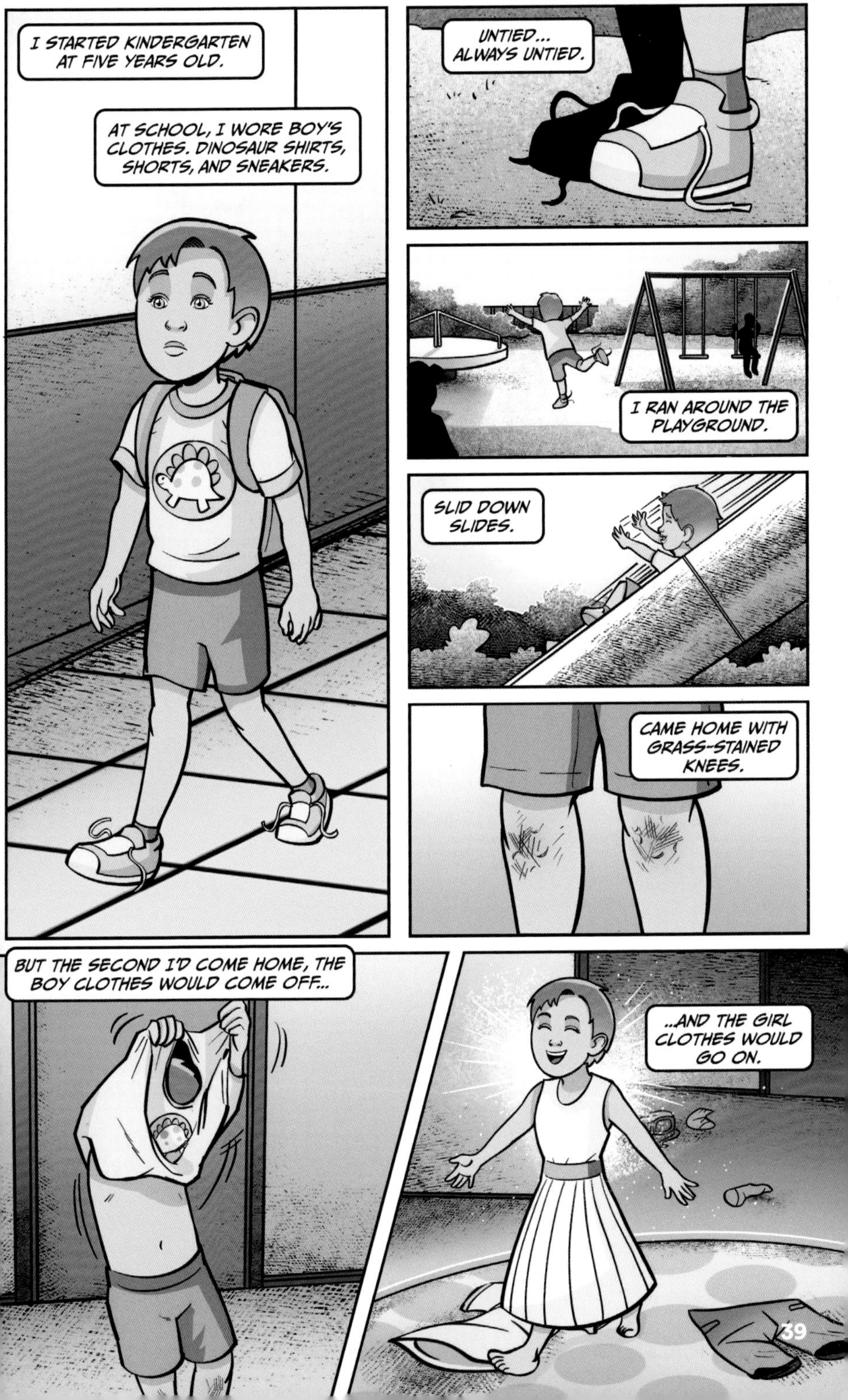
I STARTED KINDERGARTEN AT FIVE YEARS OLD.
AT SCHOOL, I WORE BOY'S CLOTHES. DINOSAUR SHIRTS, SHORTS, AND SNEAKERS.
UNTIED... ALWAYS UNTIED.
I RAN AROUND THE PLAYGROUND.
SLID DOWN SLIDES.
CAME HOME WITH GRASS-STAINED KNEES.
BUT THE SECOND I'D COME HOME, THE BOY CLOTHES WOULD COME OFF...
...AND THE GIRL CLOTHES WOULD GO ON.

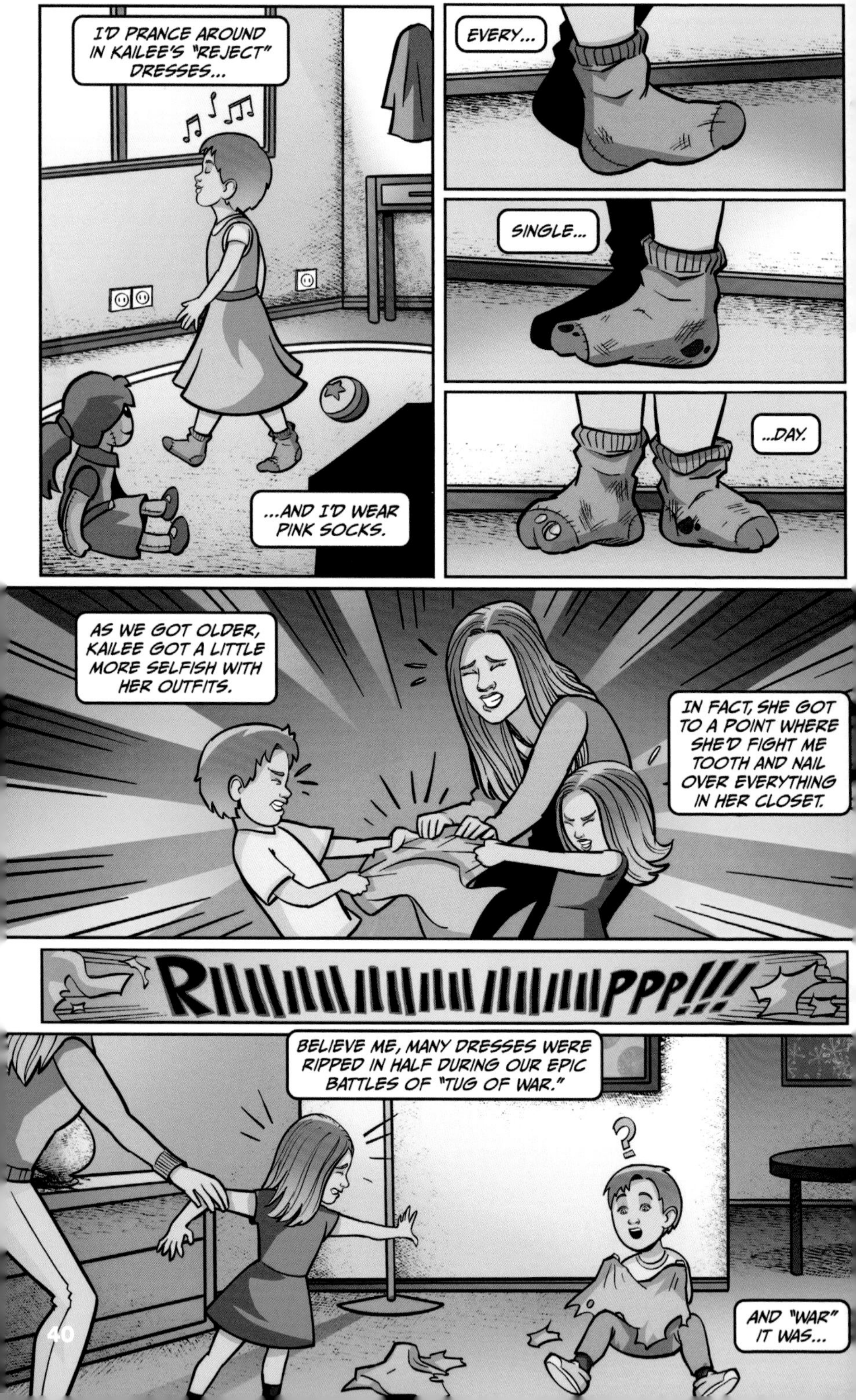
I'D PRANCE AROUND IN KAILEE'S "REJECT" DRESSES...
...AND I'D WEAR PINK SOCKS.
EVERY...
SINGLE...
...DAY.
AS WE GOT OLDER, KAILEE GOT A LITTLE MORE SELFISH WITH HER OUTFITS.
IN FACT, SHE GOT TO A POINT WHERE SHE'D FIGHT ME TOOTH AND NAIL OVER EVERYTHING IN HER CLOSET.
RIIIIIIIIIIIIIIIIIIIIIIIIPPP!!!
BELIEVE ME, MANY DRESSES WERE RIPPED IN HALF DURING OUR EPIC BATTLES OF "TUG OF WAR."
?
AND "WAR" IT WAS...

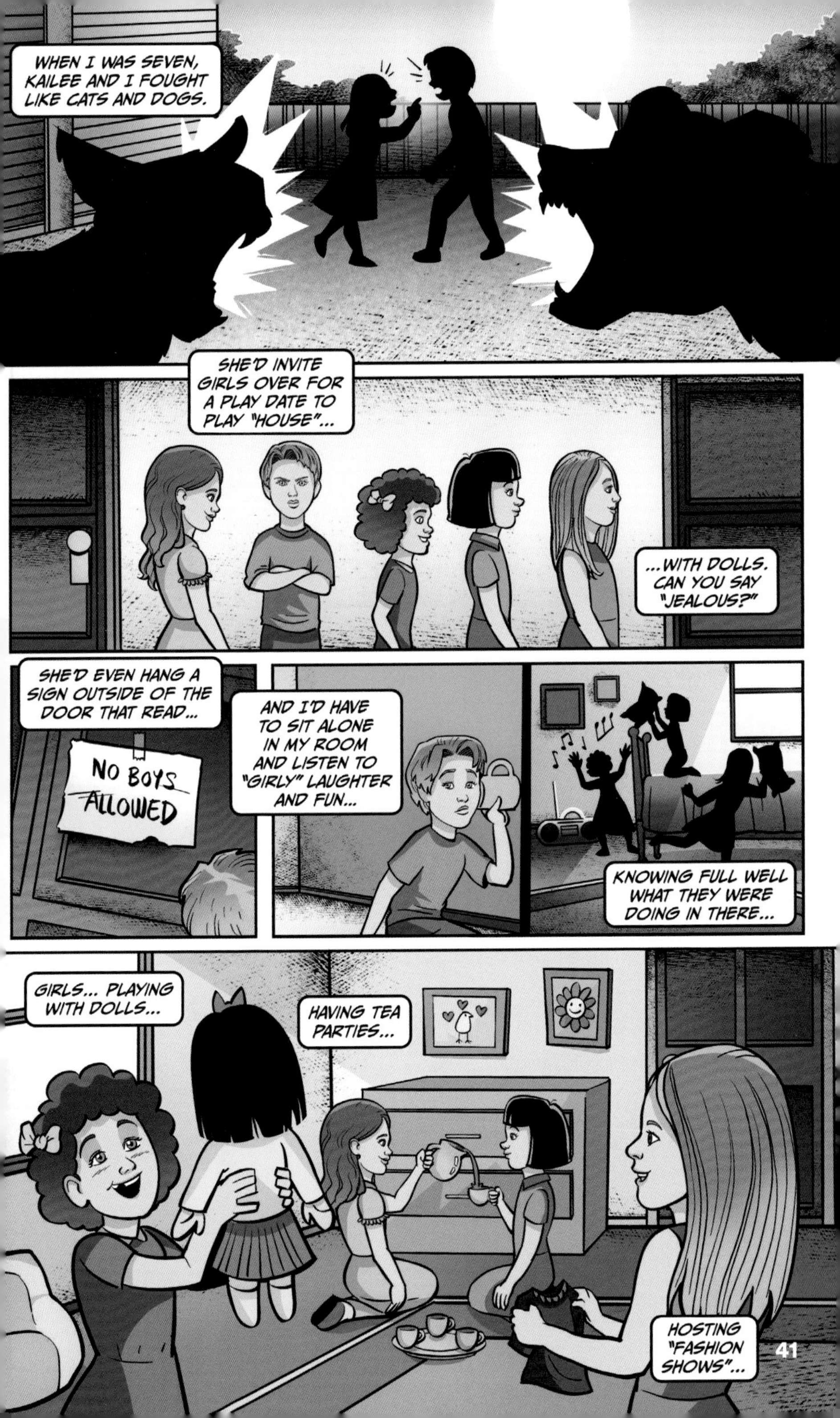
WHEN I WAS SEVEN, KAILEE AND I FOUGHT LIKE CATS AND DOGS.
SHE'D INVITE GIRLS OVER FOR A PLAY DATE TO PLAY "HOUSE"...
...WITH DOLLS. CAN YOU SAY "JEALOUS?"
SHE'D EVEN HANG A SIGN OUTSIDE OF THE DOOR THAT READ...
NO BOYS ALLOWED
AND I'D HAVE TO SIT ALONE IN MY ROOM AND LISTEN TO "GIRLY" LAUGHTER AND FUN...
KNOWING FULL WELL WHAT THEY WERE DOING IN THERE...
GIRLS... PLAYING WITH DOLLS...
HAVING TEA PARTIES...
HOSTING "FASHION SHOWS"...

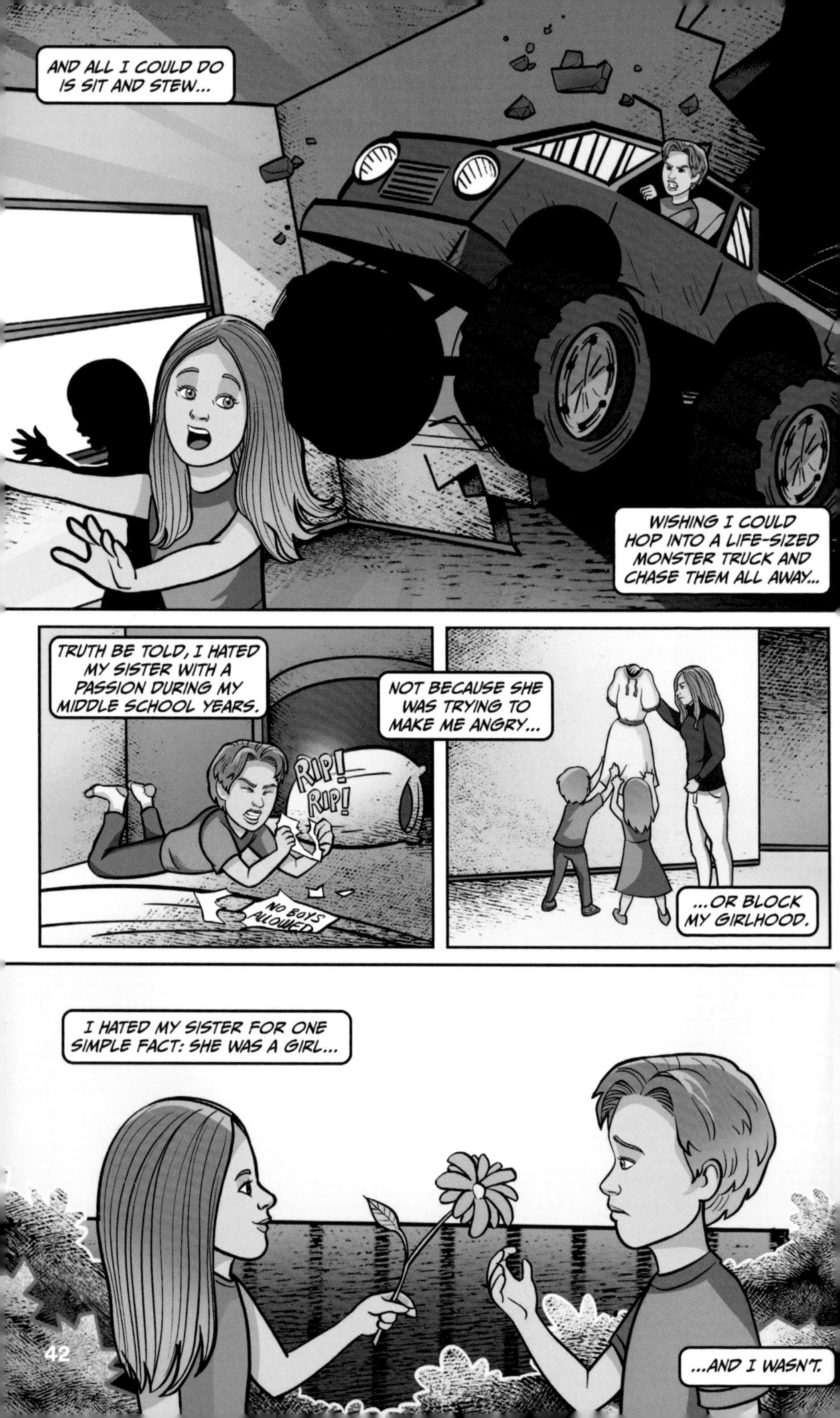

AND ALL I COULD DO IS SIT AND STEW...
WISHING I COULD HOP INTO A LIFE-SIZED MONSTER TRUCK AND CHASE THEM ALL AWAY...
TRUTH BE TOLD, I HATED MY SISTER WITH A PASSION DURING MY MIDDLE SCHOOL YEARS.
RIP! RIP!
NO BOYS ALLOWED
NOT BECAUSE SHE WAS TRYING TO MAKE ME ANGRY...
...OR BLOCK MY GIRLHOOD.
I HATED MY SISTER FOR ONE SIMPLE FACT: SHE WAS A GIRL...
...AND I WASN'T.

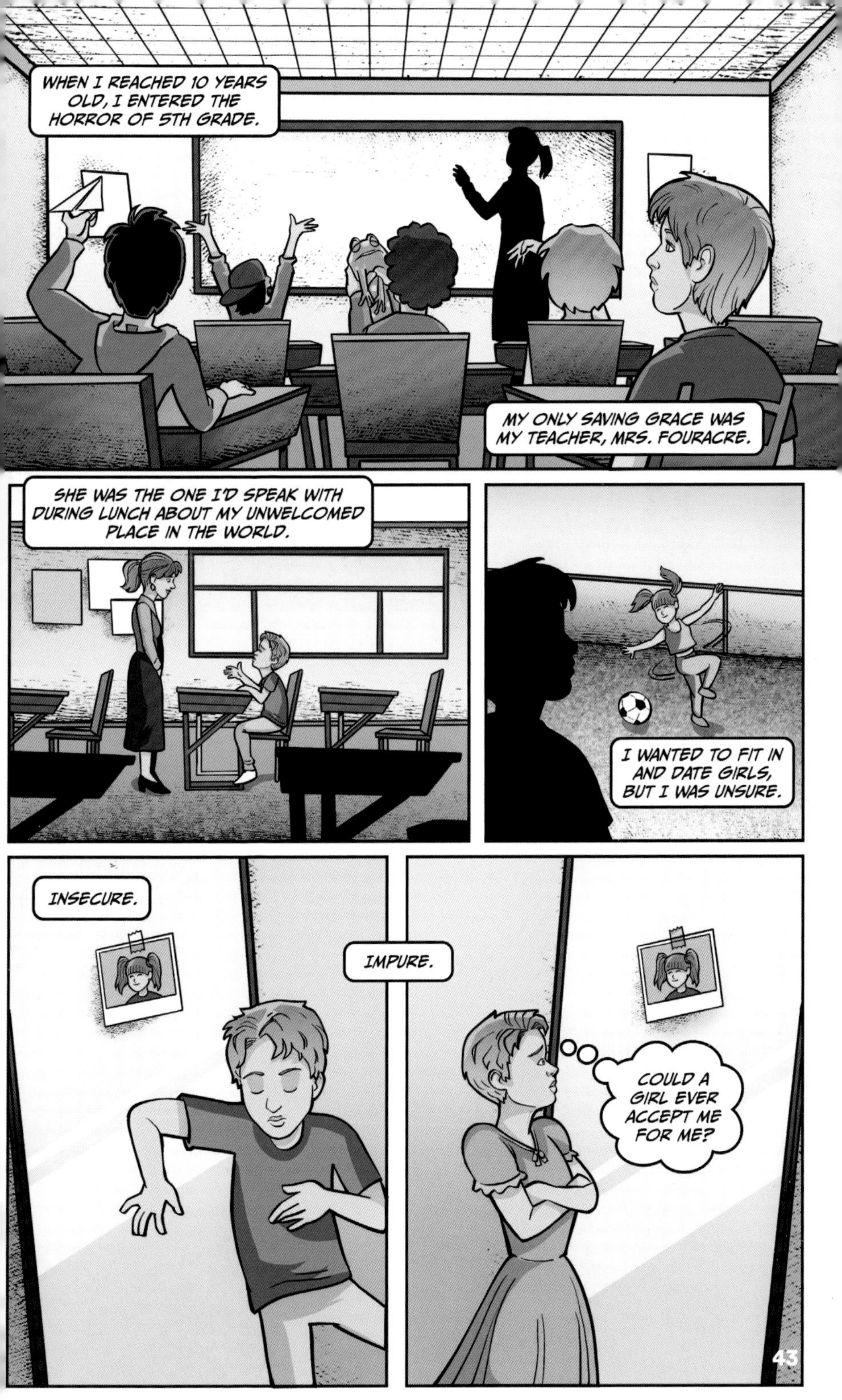

WHEN I REACHED 10 YEARS OLD, I ENTERED THE HORROR OF 5TH GRADE.
MY ONLY SAVING GRACE WAS MY TEACHER, MRS. FOURACRE.
SHE WAS THE ONE I'D SPEAK WITH DURING LUNCH ABOUT MY UNWELCOMED PLACE IN THE WORLD.
I WANTED TO FIT IN AND DATE GIRLS, BUT I WAS UNSURE.
INSECURE.
IMPURE.
COULD A GIRL EVER ACCEPT ME FOR ME?

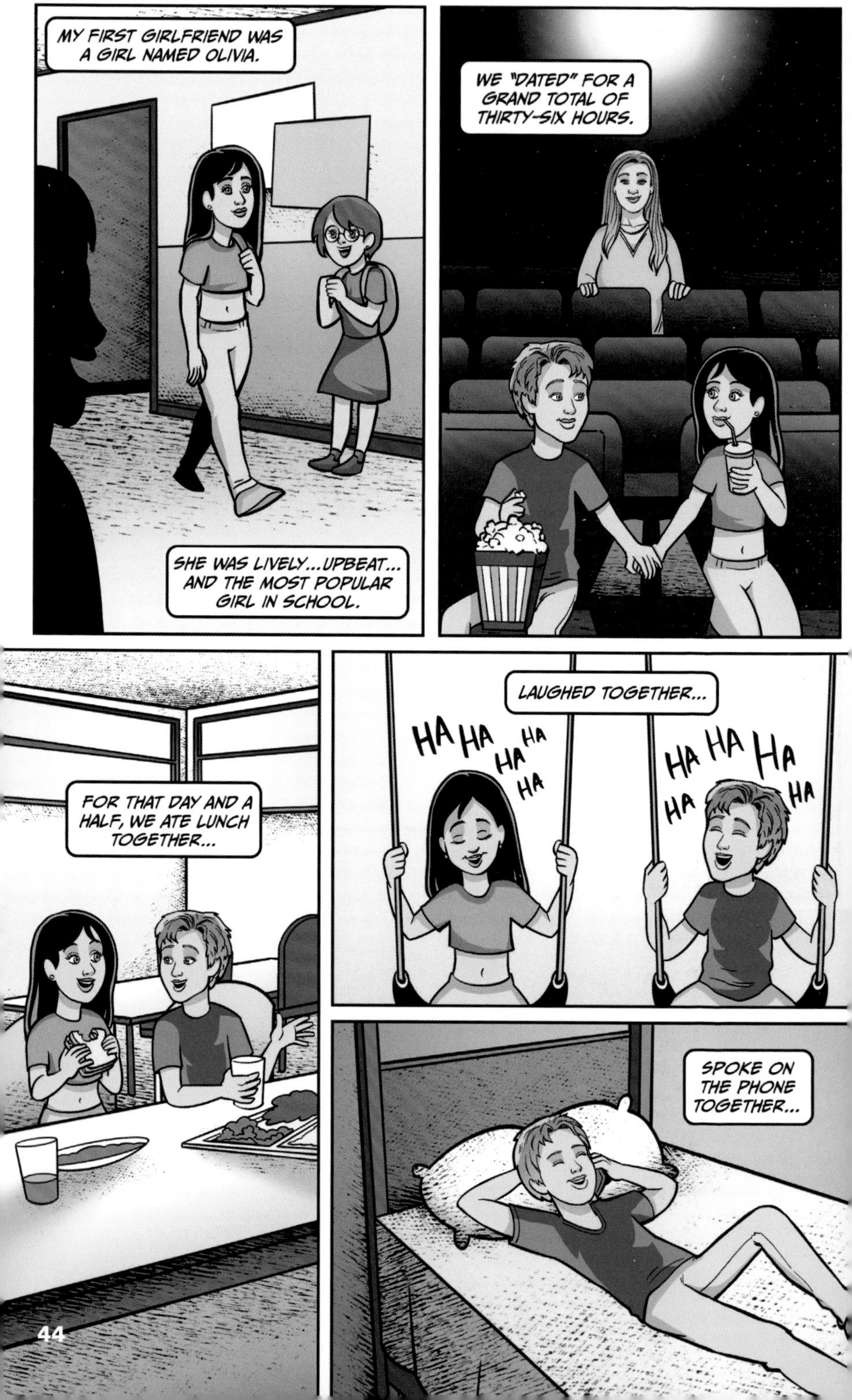
MY FIRST GIRLFRIEND WAS A GIRL NAMED OLIVIA.
SHE WAS LIVELY...UPBEAT... AND THE MOST POPULAR GIRL IN SCHOOL.
WE "DATED" FOR A GRAND TOTAL OF THIRTY-SIX HOURS.
FOR THAT DAY AND A HALF, WE ATE LUNCH TOGETHER...
LAUGHED TOGETHER...
HA HA HA HA HA HA
HA HA HA HA HA HA
SPOKE ON THE PHONE TOGETHER...

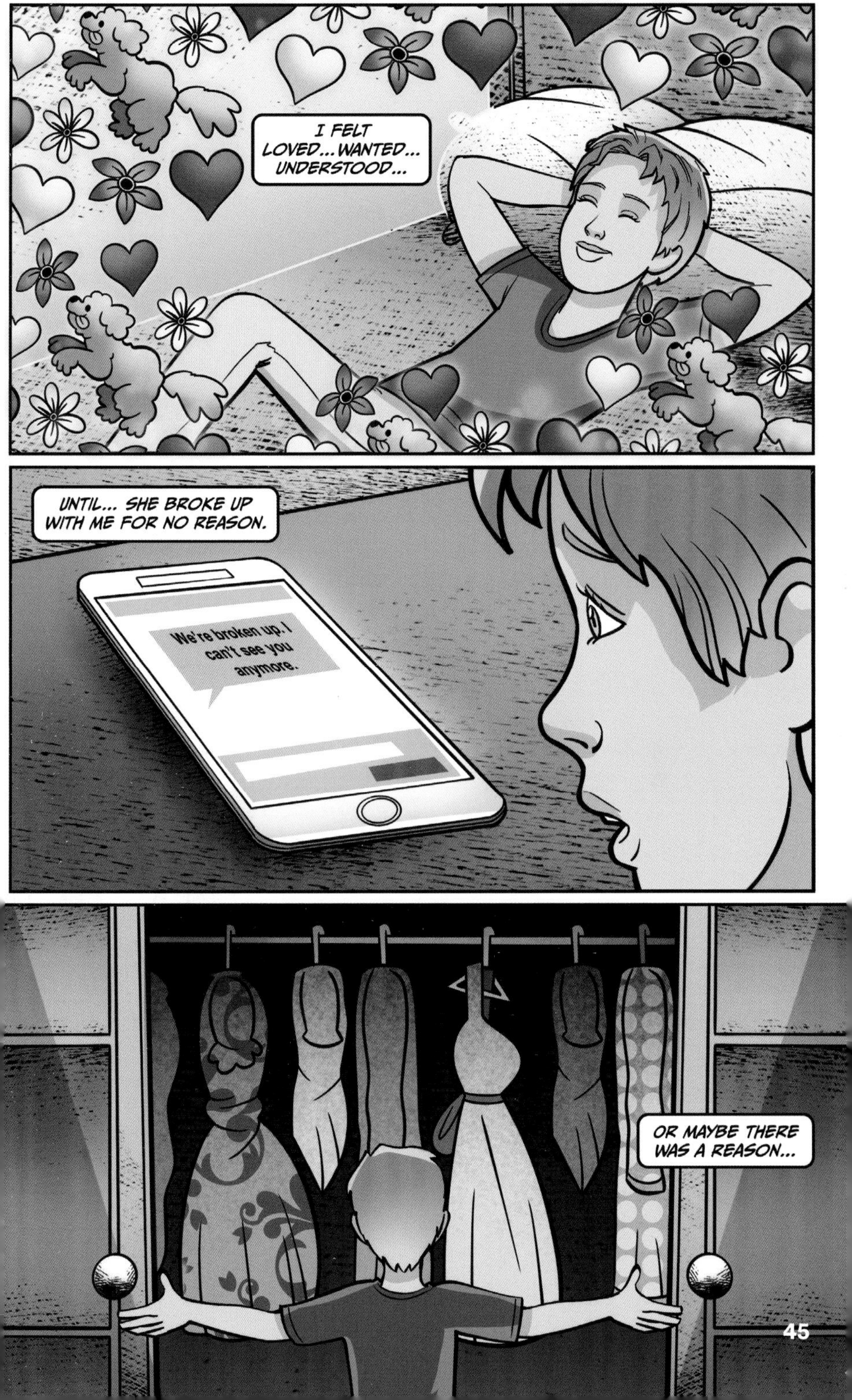
I FELT LOVED... WANTED... UNDERSTOOD...
UNTIL... SHE BROKE UP WITH ME FOR NO REASON.
We're broken up. I can't see you anymore.
OR MAYBE THERE WAS A REASON...

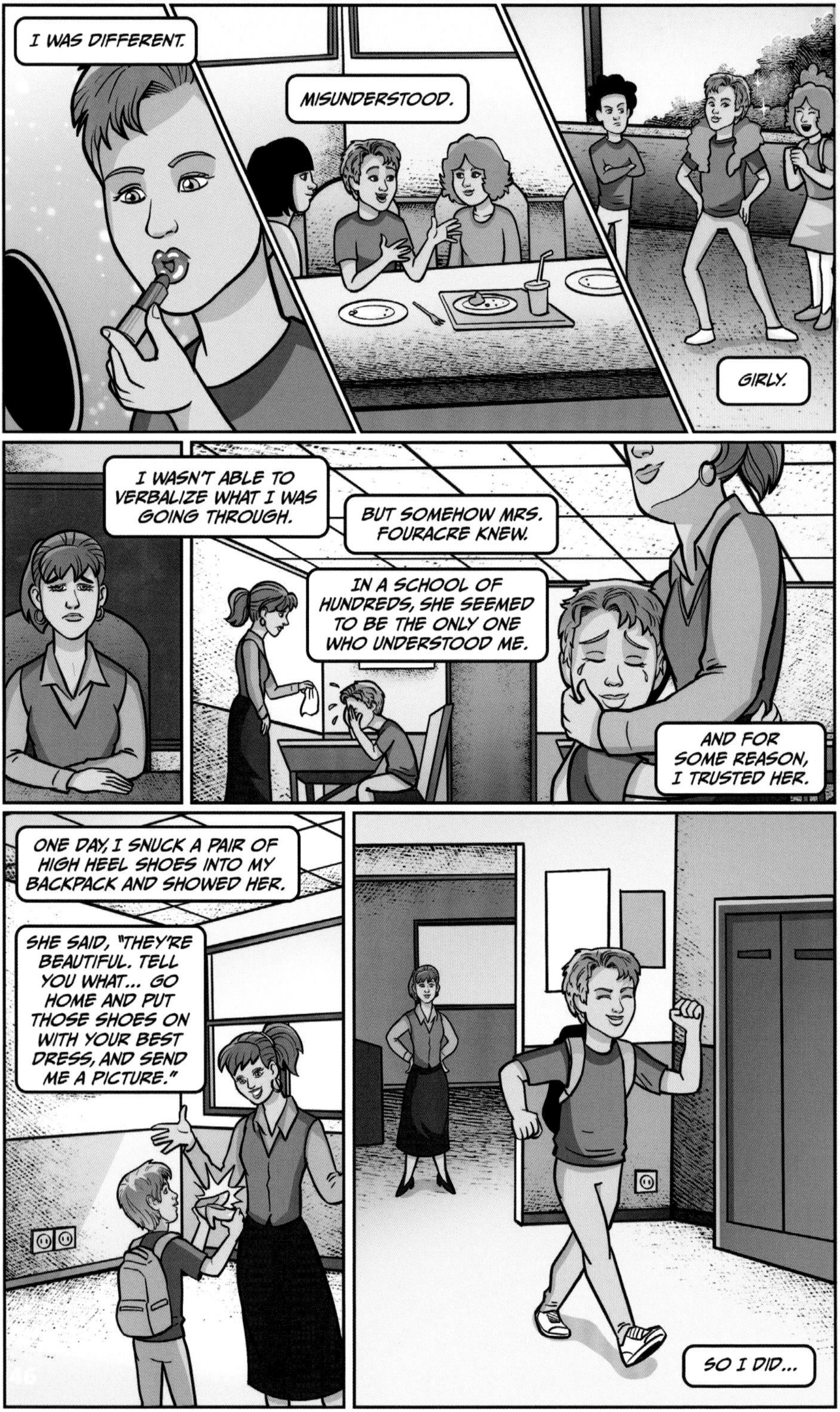
I WAS DIFFERENT.
MISUNDERSTOOD.
GIRLY.
I WASN'T ABLE TO VERBALIZE WHAT I WAS GOING THROUGH.
BUT SOMEHOW MRS. FOURACRE KNEW.
IN A SCHOOL OF HUNDREDS, SHE SEEMED TO BE THE ONLY ONE WHO UNDERSTOOD ME.
AND FOR SOME REASON, I TRUSTED HER.
ONE DAY, I SNUCK A PAIR OF HIGH HEEL SHOES INTO MY BACKPACK AND SHOWED HER.
SHE SAID, "THEY'RE BEAUTIFUL. TELL YOU WHAT... GO HOME AND PUT THOSE SHOES ON WITH YOUR BEST DRESS, AND SEND ME A PICTURE."
SO I DID...

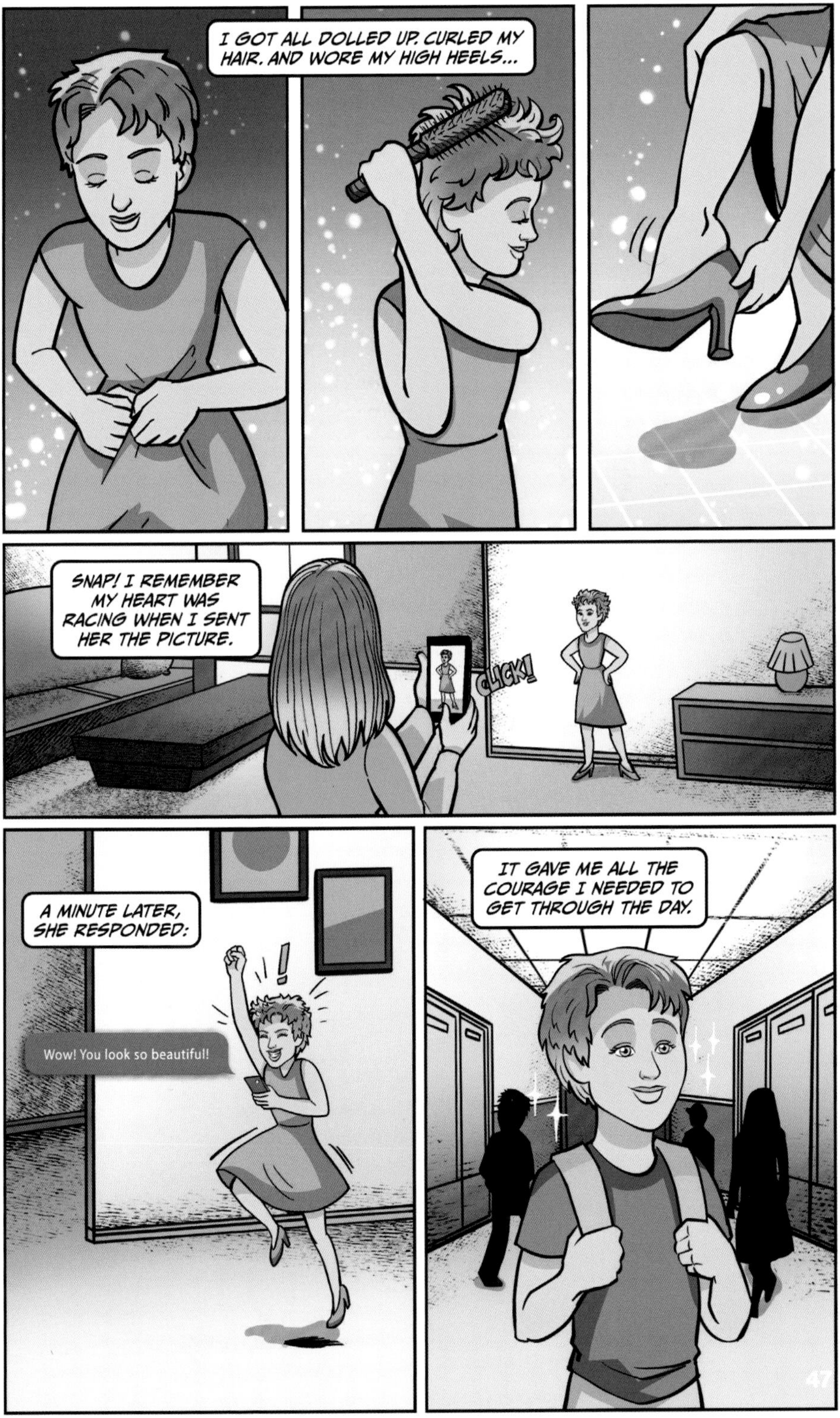
I GOT ALL DOLLED UP. CURLED MY HAIR. AND WORE MY HIGH HEELS...
SNAP! I REMEMBER MY HEART WAS RACING WHEN I SENT HER THE PICTURE.
CLICK!
A MINUTE LATER, SHE RESPONDED:
Wow! You look so beautiful!
!
IT GAVE ME ALL THE COURAGE I NEEDED TO GET THROUGH THE DAY.

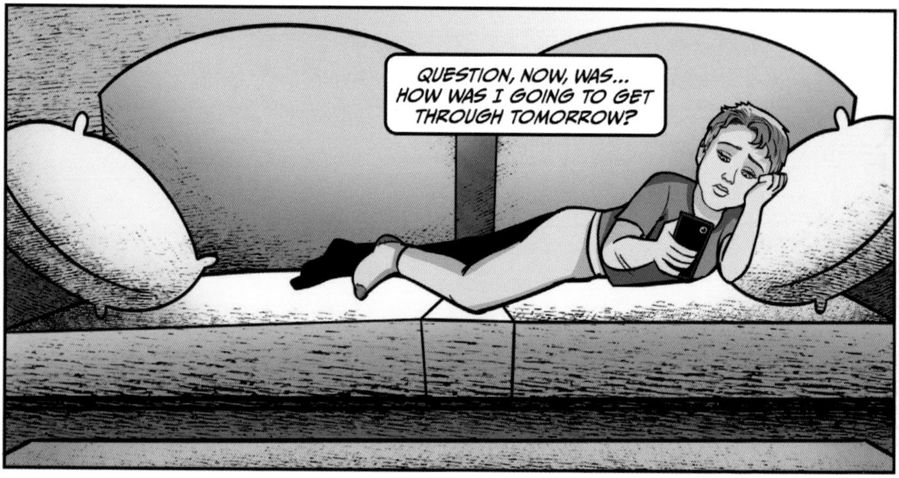
QUESTION, NOW, WAS... HOW WAS I GOING TO GET THROUGH TOMORROW?

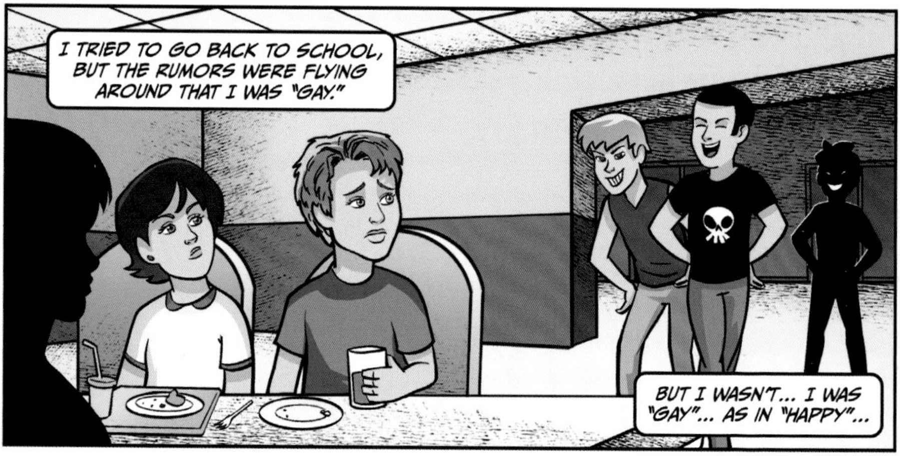
I TRIED TO GO BACK TO SCHOOL, BUT THE RUMORS WERE FLYING AROUND THAT I WAS "GAY."
BUT I WASN'T... I WAS "GAY"... AS IN "HAPPY"...

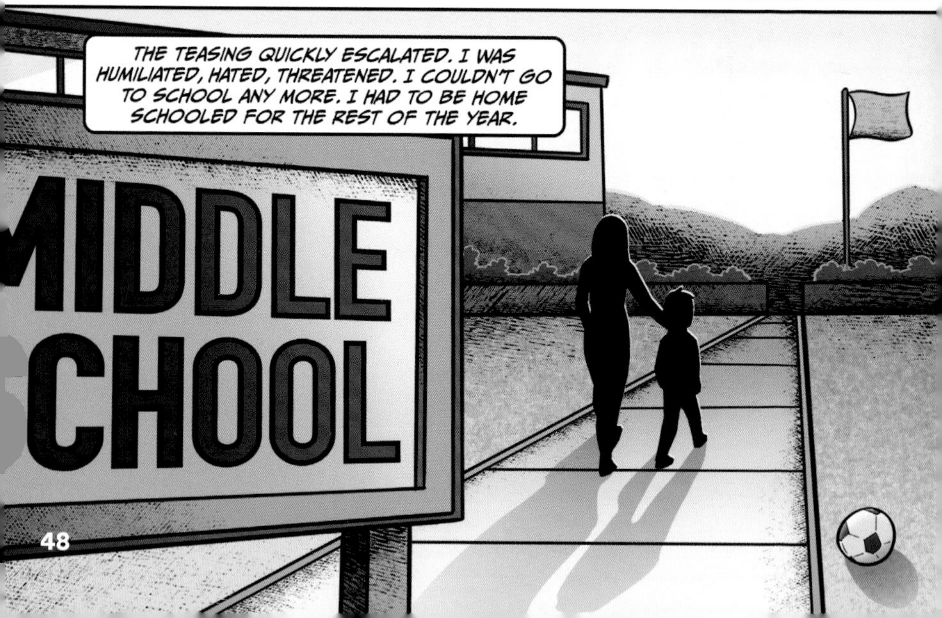
THE TEASING QUICKLY ESCALATED. I WAS HUMILIATED, HATED, THREATENED. I COULDN'T GO TO SCHOOL ANY MORE. I HAD TO BE HOME SCHOOLED FOR THE REST OF THE YEAR.
MIDDLE
CHOOL

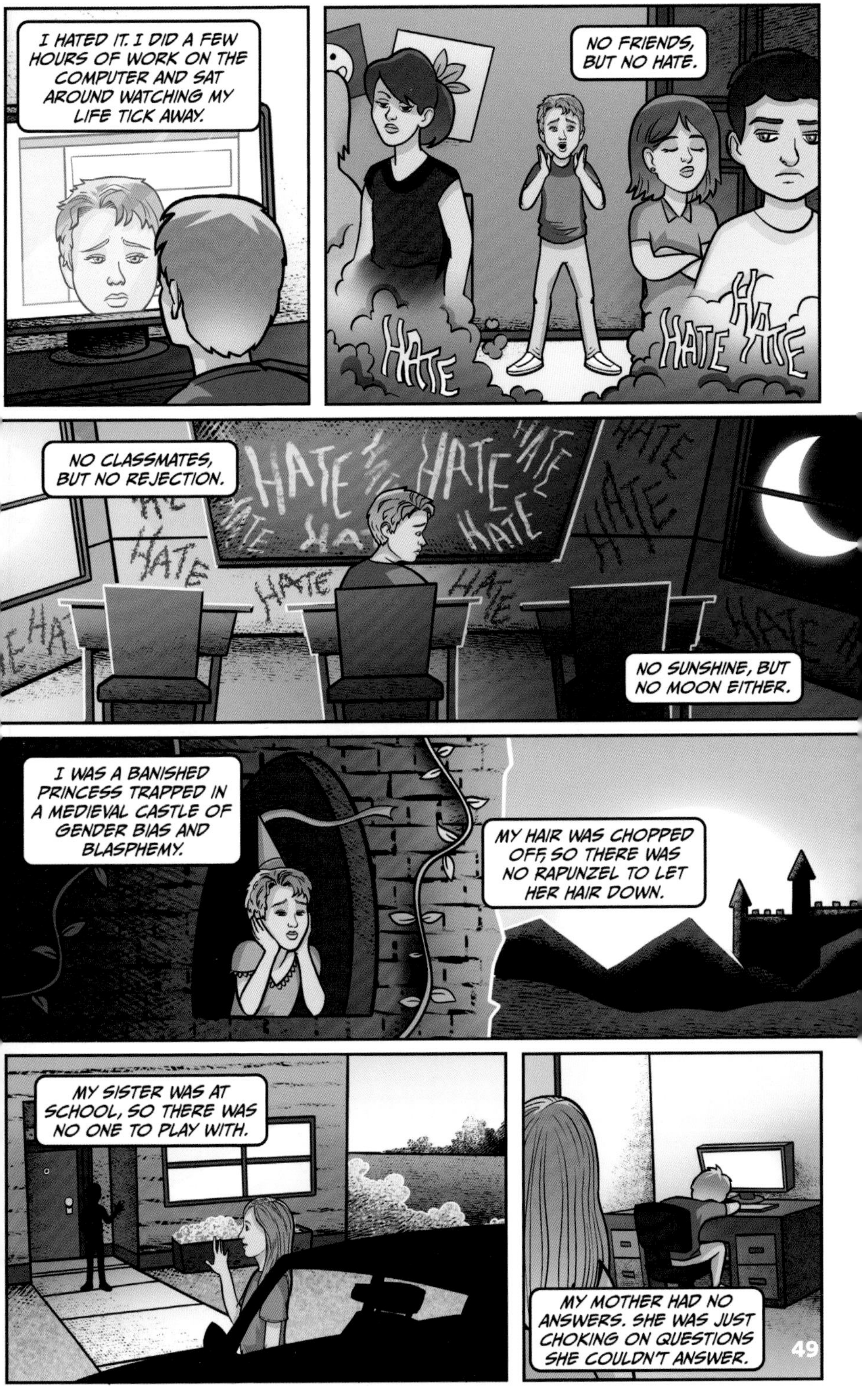

I HATED IT. I DID A FEW HOURS OF WORK ON THE COMPUTER AND SAT AROUND WATCHING MY LIFE TICK AWAY.
NO FRIENDS, BUT NO HATE.
HATE
HATE
HATE
HATE
NO CLASSMATES, BUT NO REJECTION.
HATE
HATE
HATE
HATE
HATE
NO SUNSHINE, BUT NO MOON EITHER.
I WAS A BANISHED PRINCESS TRAPPED IN A MEDIEVAL CASTLE OF GENDER BIAS AND BLASPHEMY.
MY HAIR WAS CHOPPED OFF, SO THERE WAS NO RAPUNZEL TO LET HER HAIR DOWN.
MY SISTER WAS AT SCHOOL, SO THERE WAS NO ONE TO PLAY WITH.
MY MOTHER HAD NO ANSWERS. SHE WAS JUST CHOKING ON QUESTIONS SHE COULDN'T ANSWER.

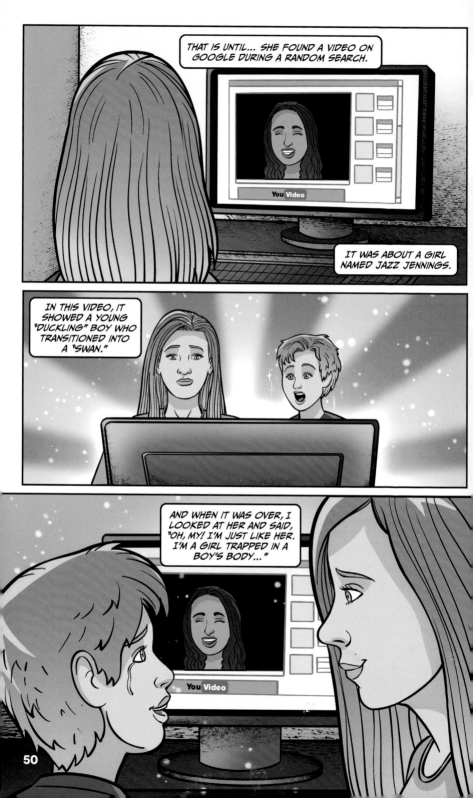

THAT IS UNTIL... SHE FOUND A VIDEO ON GOOGLE DURING A RANDOM SEARCH.

You Video

IT WAS ABOUT A GIRL NAMED JAZZ JENNINGS.

IN THIS VIDEO, IT SHOWED A YOUNG "DUCKLING" BOY WHO TRANSITIONED INTO A "SWAN."

AND WHEN IT WAS OVER, I LOOKED AT HER AND SAID, "OH, MY! I'M JUST LIKE HER. I'M A GIRL TRAPPED IN A BOY'S BODY..."

You Video

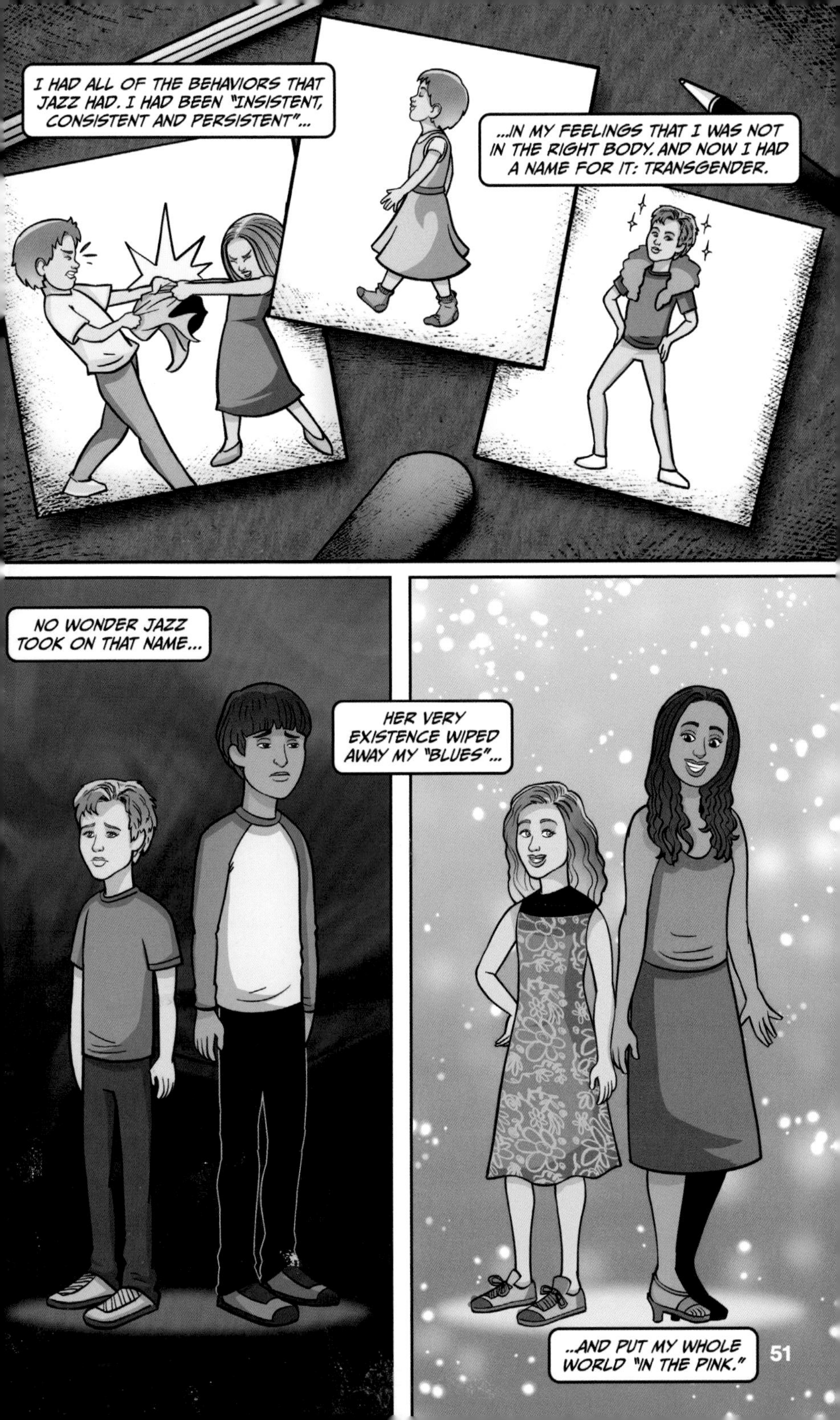

I HAD ALL OF THE BEHAVIORS THAT JAZZ HAD. I HAD BEEN "INSISTENT, CONSISTENT AND PERSISTENT"...
...IN MY FEELINGS THAT I WAS NOT IN THE RIGHT BODY. AND NOW I HAD A NAME FOR IT: TRANSGENDER.
NO WONDER JAZZ TOOK ON THAT NAME...
HER VERY EXISTENCE WIPED AWAY MY "BLUES"...
...AND PUT MY WHOLE WORLD "IN THE PINK."

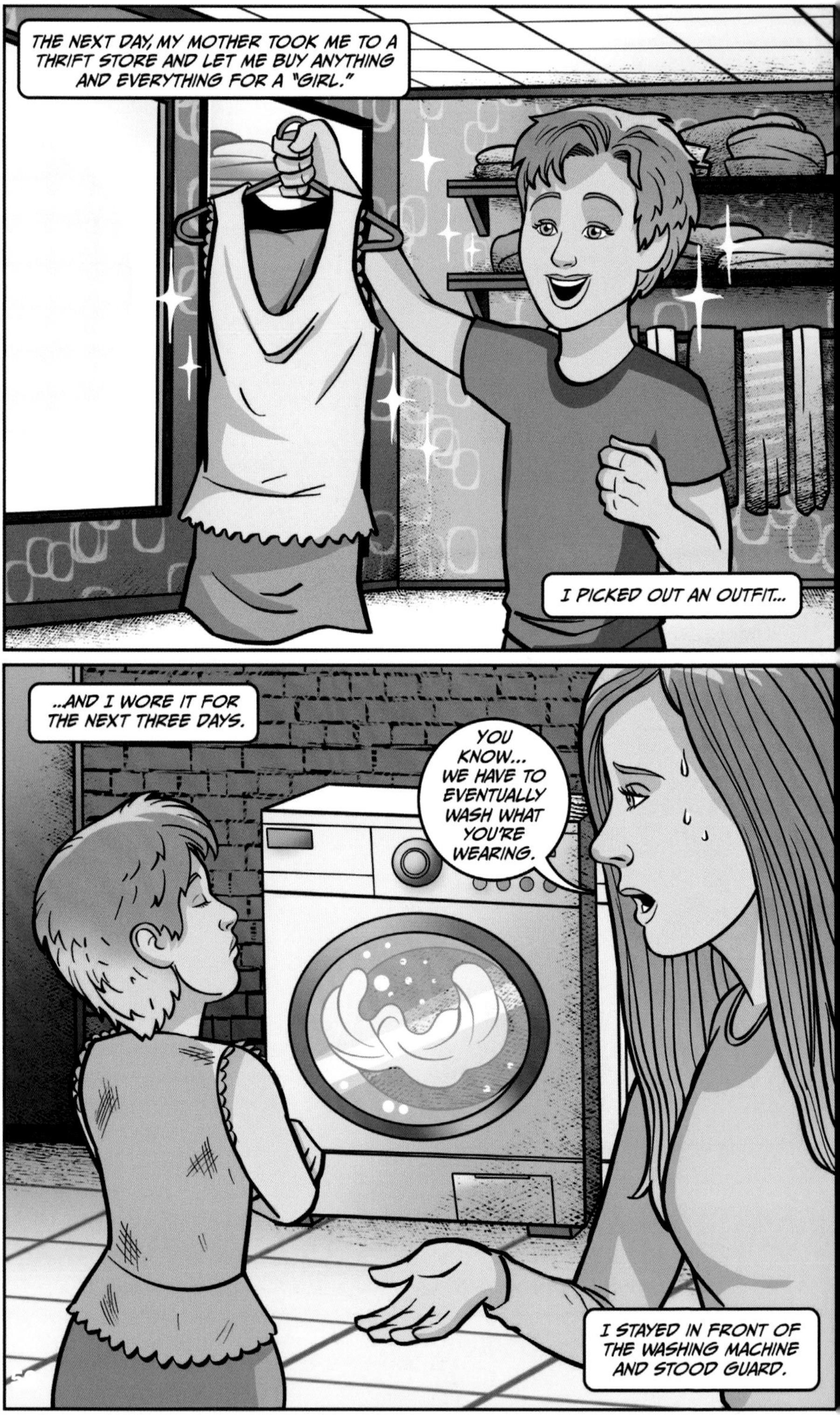
THE NEXT DAY, MY MOTHER TOOK ME TO A THRIFT STORE AND LET ME BUY ANYTHING AND EVERYTHING FOR A "GIRL."
I PICKED OUT AN OUTFIT...
..AND I WORE IT FOR THE NEXT THREE DAYS.
YOU KNOW... WE HAVE TO EVENTUALLY WASH WHAT YOU'RE WEARING.
I STAYED IN FRONT OF THE WASHING MACHINE AND STOOD GUARD.

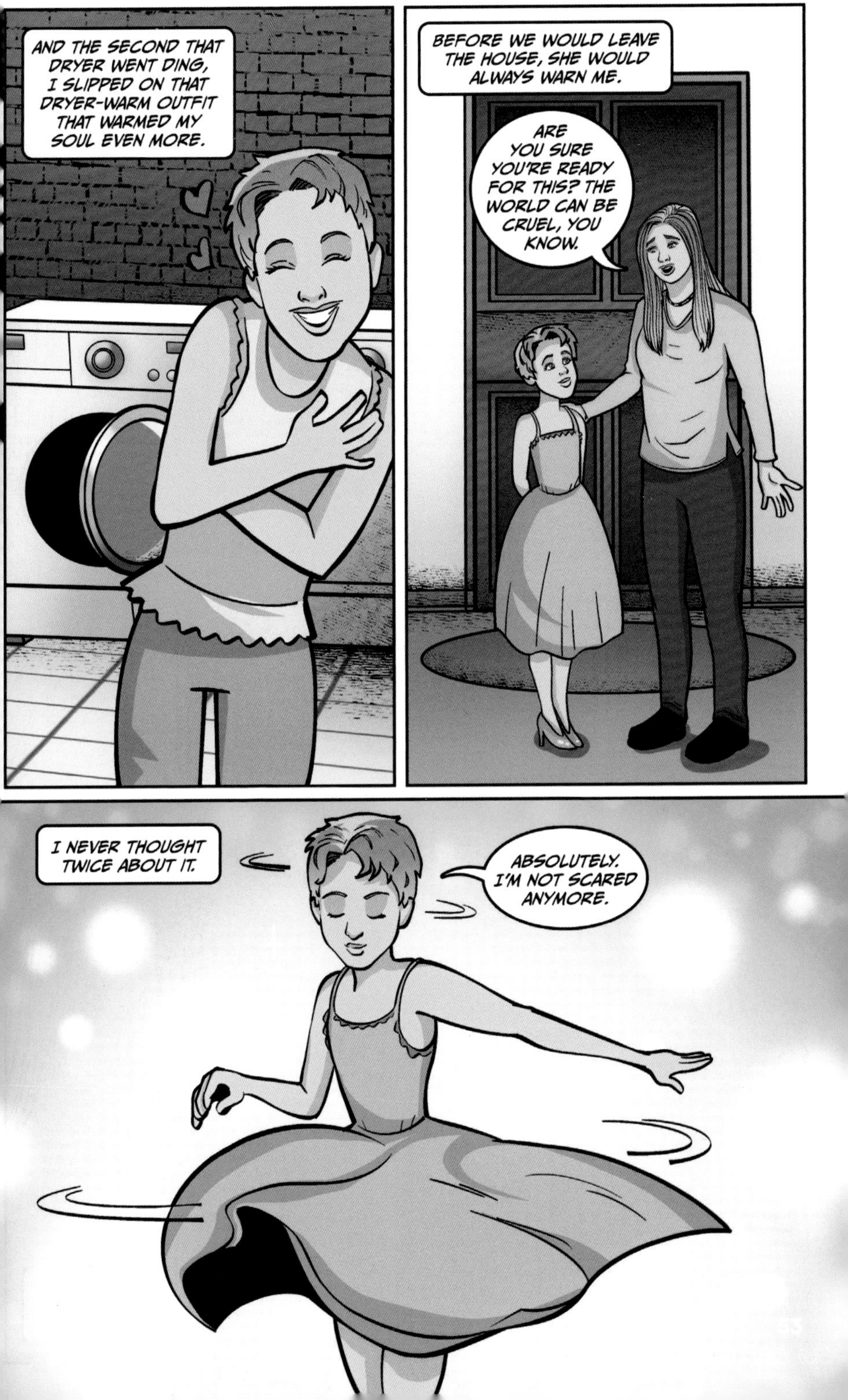
AND THE SECOND THAT DRYER WENT DING, I SLIPPED ON THAT DRYER-WARM OUTFIT THAT WARMED MY SOUL EVEN MORE.
BEFORE WE WOULD LEAVE THE HOUSE, SHE WOULD ALWAYS WARN ME.
ARE YOU SURE YOU'RE READY FOR THIS? THE WORLD CAN BE CRUEL, YOU KNOW.
I NEVER THOUGHT TWICE ABOUT IT.
ABSOLUTELY. I'M NOT SCARED ANYMORE.

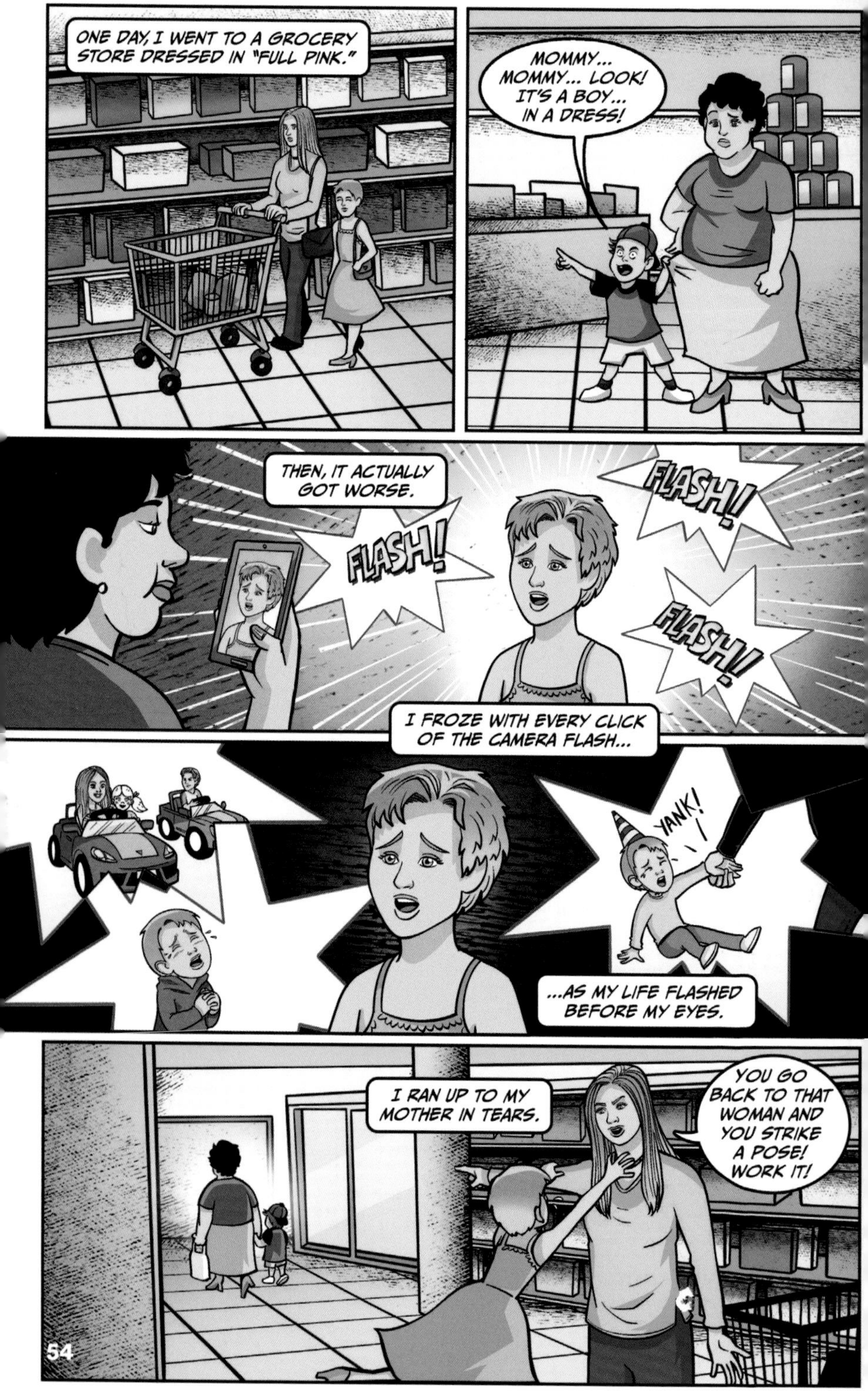

ONE DAY, I WENT TO A GROCERY STORE DRESSED IN "FULL PINK."
MOMMY... MOMMY... LOOK! IT'S A BOY... IN A DRESS!
THEN, IT ACTUALLY GOT WORSE.
FLASH!
FLASH!!
FLASH!!
I FROZE WITH EVERY CLICK OF THE CAMERA FLASH...
YANK!
...AS MY LIFE FLASHED BEFORE MY EYES.
I RAN UP TO MY MOTHER IN TEARS.
YOU GO BACK TO THAT WOMAN AND YOU STRIKE A POSE! WORK IT!

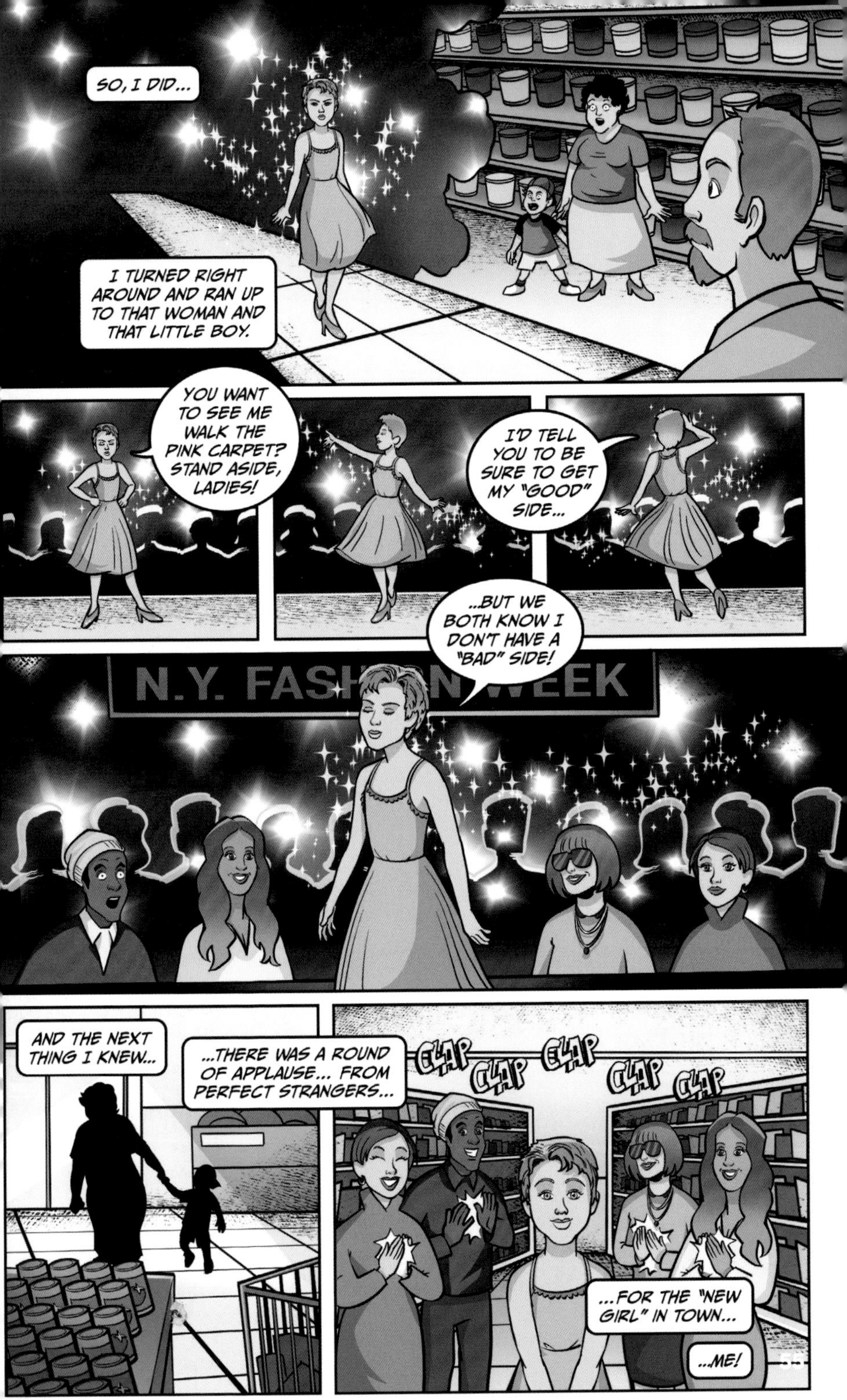

SO, I DID...
I TURNED RIGHT AROUND AND RAN UP TO THAT WOMAN AND THAT LITTLE BOY.
YOU WANT TO SEE ME WALK THE PINK CARPET? STAND ASIDE, LADIES!
I'D TELL YOU TO BE SURE TO GET MY "GOOD" SIDE...
...BUT WE BOTH KNOW I DON'T HAVE A "BAD" SIDE!
N.Y. FASH N WEEK
AND THE NEXT THING I KNEW...
...THERE WAS A ROUND OF APPLAUSE... FROM PERFECT STRANGERS...
CLAP CLAP CLAP CLAP CLAP
...FOR THE "NEW GIRL" IN TOWN...
...ME!

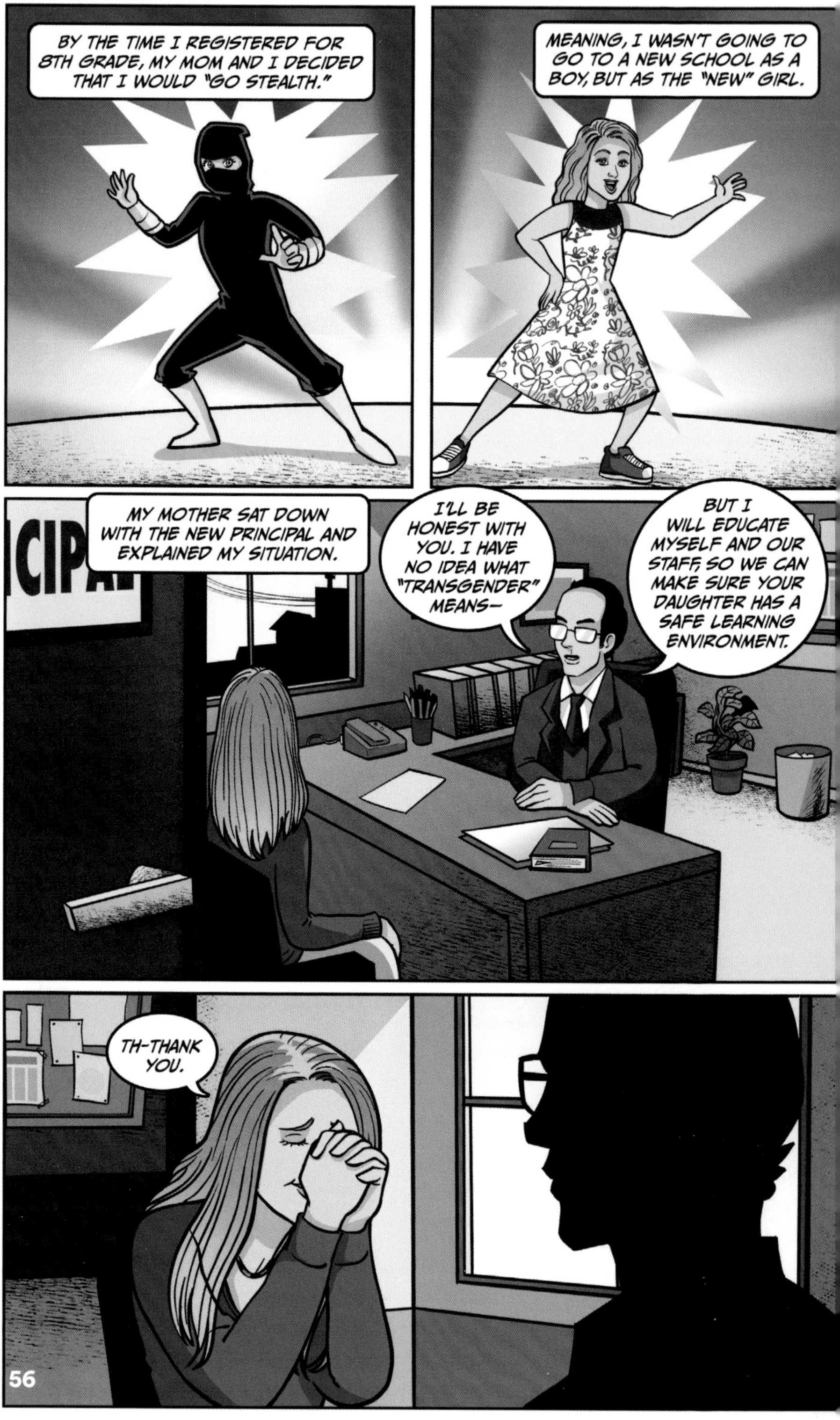
BY THE TIME I REGISTERED FOR 8TH GRADE, MY MOM AND I DECIDED THAT I WOULD "GO STEALTH."
MEANING, I WASN'T GOING TO GO TO A NEW SCHOOL AS A BOY, BUT AS THE "NEW" GIRL.
MY MOTHER SAT DOWN WITH THE NEW PRINCIPAL AND EXPLAINED MY SITUATION.
I'LL BE HONEST WITH YOU. I HAVE NO IDEA WHAT "TRANSGENDER" MEANS—
BUT I WILL EDUCATE MYSELF AND OUR STAFF, SO WE CAN MAKE SURE YOUR DAUGHTER HAS A SAFE LEARNING ENVIRONMENT.
TH-THANK YOU.

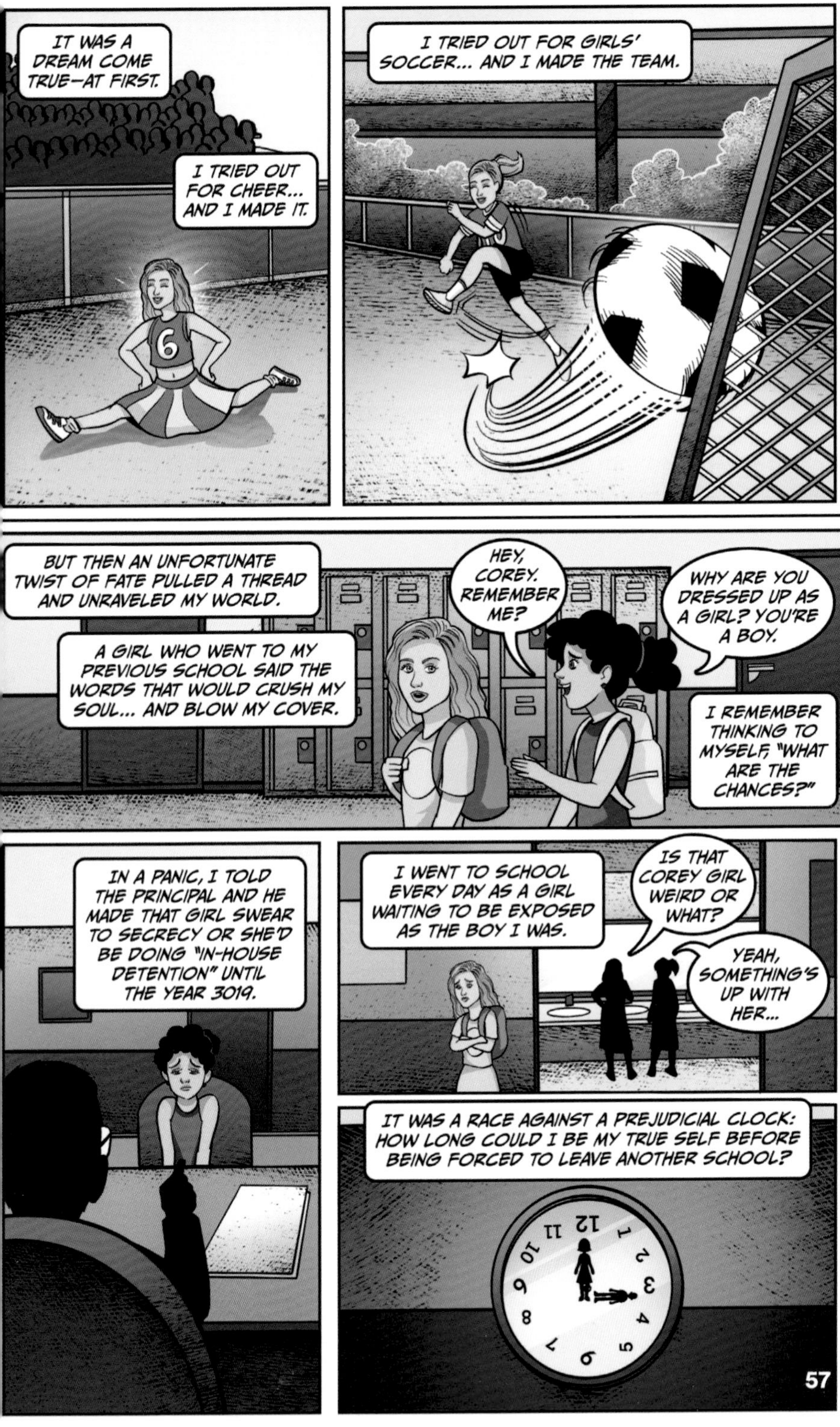
IT WAS A DREAM COME TRUE—AT FIRST.
I TRIED OUT FOR CHEER... AND I MADE IT.
6
I TRIED OUT FOR GIRLS' SOCCER... AND I MADE THE TEAM.
BUT THEN AN UNFORTUNATE TWIST OF FATE PULLED A THREAD AND UNRAVELED MY WORLD.
A GIRL WHO WENT TO MY PREVIOUS SCHOOL SAID THE WORDS THAT WOULD CRUSH MY SOUL... AND BLOW MY COVER.
HEY, COREY. REMEMBER ME?
WHY ARE YOU DRESSED UP AS A GIRL? YOU'RE A BOY.
I REMEMBER THINKING TO MYSELF, "WHAT ARE THE CHANCES?"
IN A PANIC, I TOLD THE PRINCIPAL AND HE MADE THAT GIRL SWEAR TO SECRECY OR SHE'D BE DOING "IN-HOUSE DETENTION" UNTIL THE YEAR 3019.
I WENT TO SCHOOL EVERY DAY AS A GIRL WAITING TO BE EXPOSED AS THE BOY I WAS.
IS THAT COREY GIRL WEIRD OR WHAT?
YEAH, SOMETHING'S UP WITH HER...
IT WAS A RACE AGAINST A PREJUDICIAL CLOCK: HOW LONG COULD I BE MY TRUE SELF BEFORE BEING FORCED TO LEAVE ANOTHER SCHOOL?

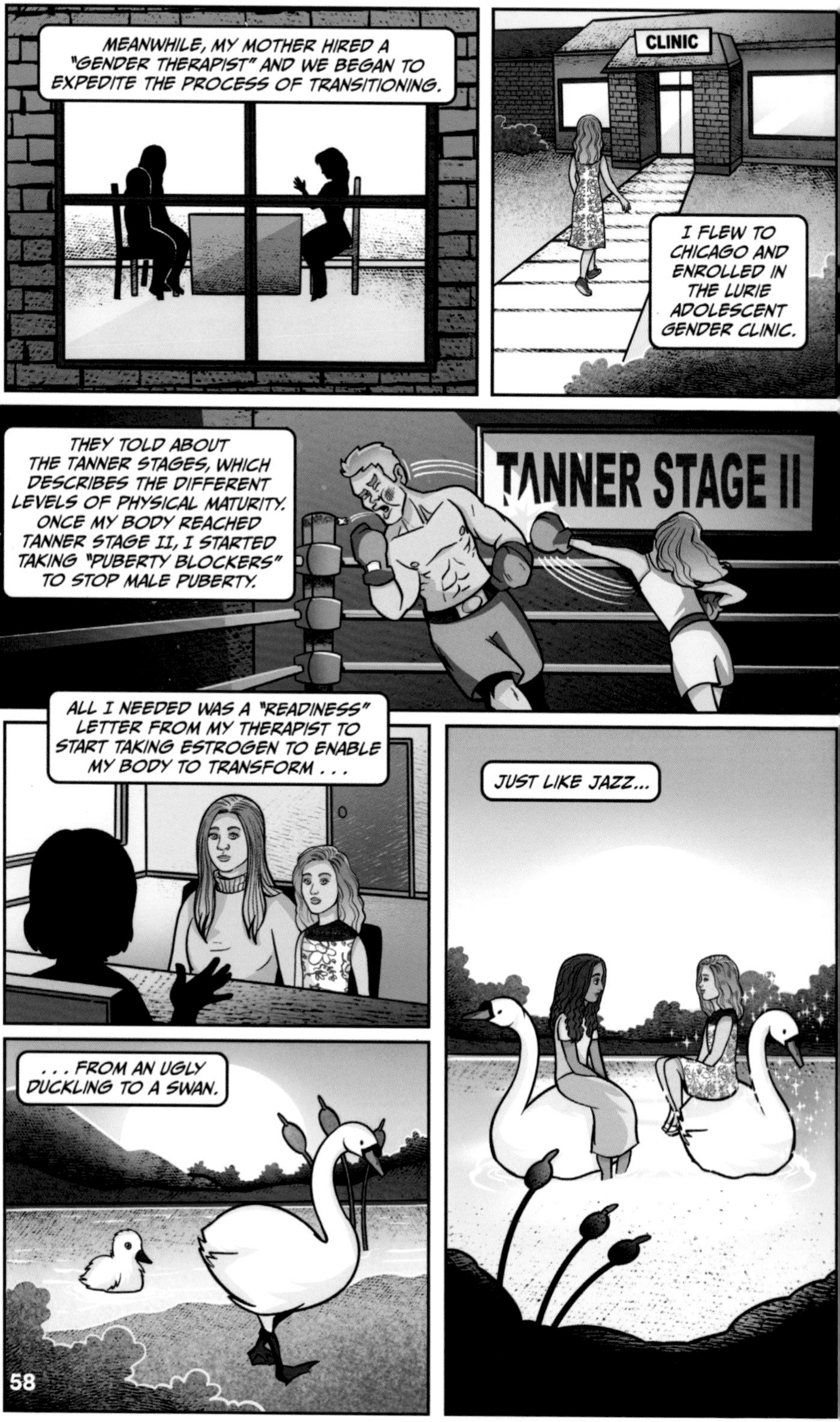
MEANWHILE, MY MOTHER HIRED A "GENDER THERAPIST" AND WE BEGAN TO EXPEDITE THE PROCESS OF TRANSITIONING.
CLINIC
I FLEW TO CHICAGO AND ENROLLED IN THE LURIE ADOLESCENT GENDER CLINIC.
THEY TOLD ABOUT THE TANNER STAGES, WHICH DESCRIBES THE DIFFERENT LEVELS OF PHYSICAL MATURITY. ONCE MY BODY REACHED TANNER STAGE II, I STARTED TAKING "PUBERTY BLOCKERS" TO STOP MALE PUBERTY.
TANNER STAGE II
ALL I NEEDED WAS A "READINESS" LETTER FROM MY THERAPIST TO START TAKING ESTROGEN TO ENABLE MY BODY TO TRANSFORM . . .
JUST LIKE JAZZ...
. . . FROM AN UGLY DUCKLING TO A SWAN.

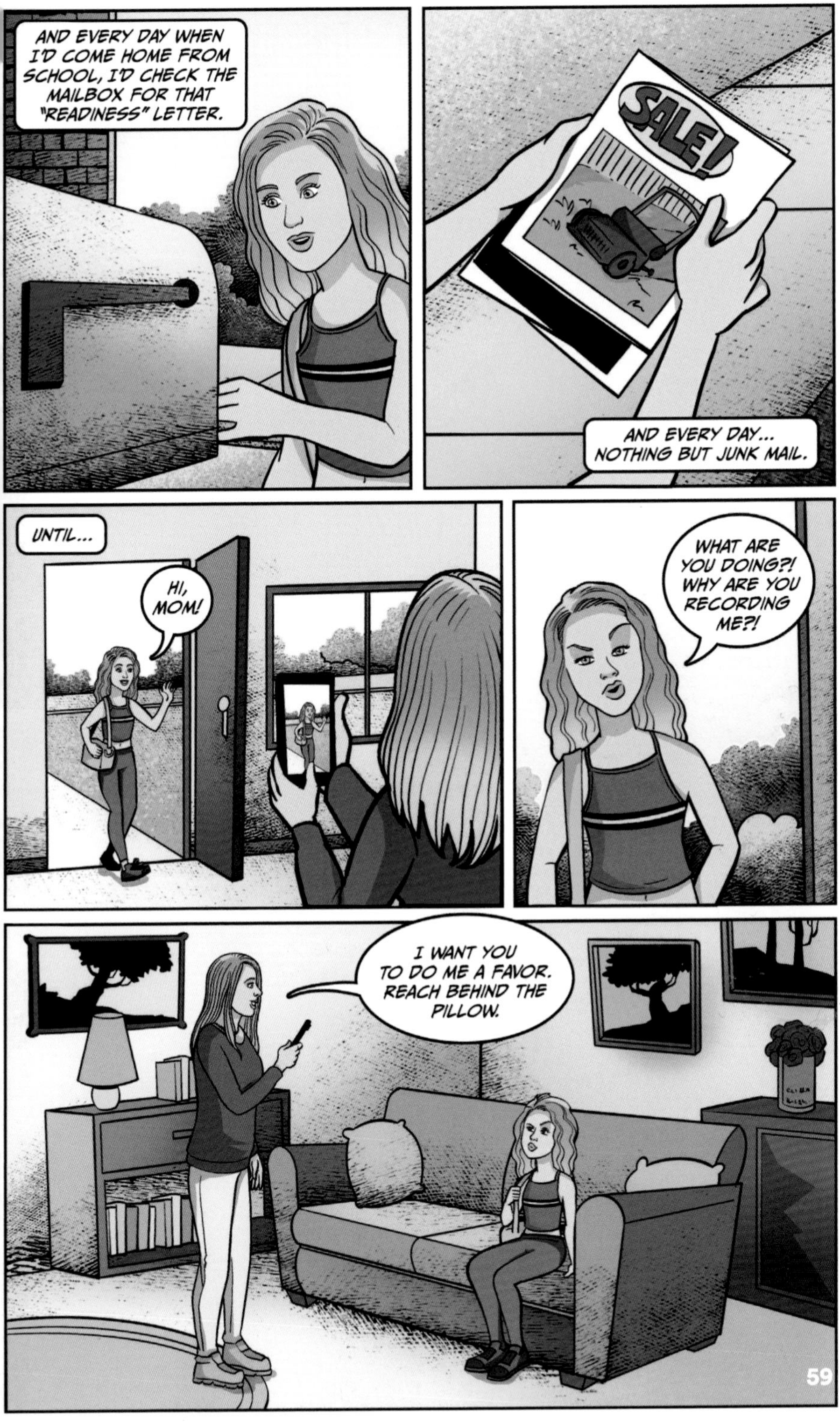
AND EVERY DAY WHEN I'D COME HOME FROM SCHOOL, I'D CHECK THE MAILBOX FOR THAT "READINESS" LETTER.
SALE!
AND EVERY DAY... NOTHING BUT JUNK MAIL.
UNTIL...
HI, MOM!
WHAT ARE YOU DOING?! WHY ARE YOU RECORDING ME?!
I WANT YOU TO DO ME A FAVOR. REACH BEHIND THE PILLOW.

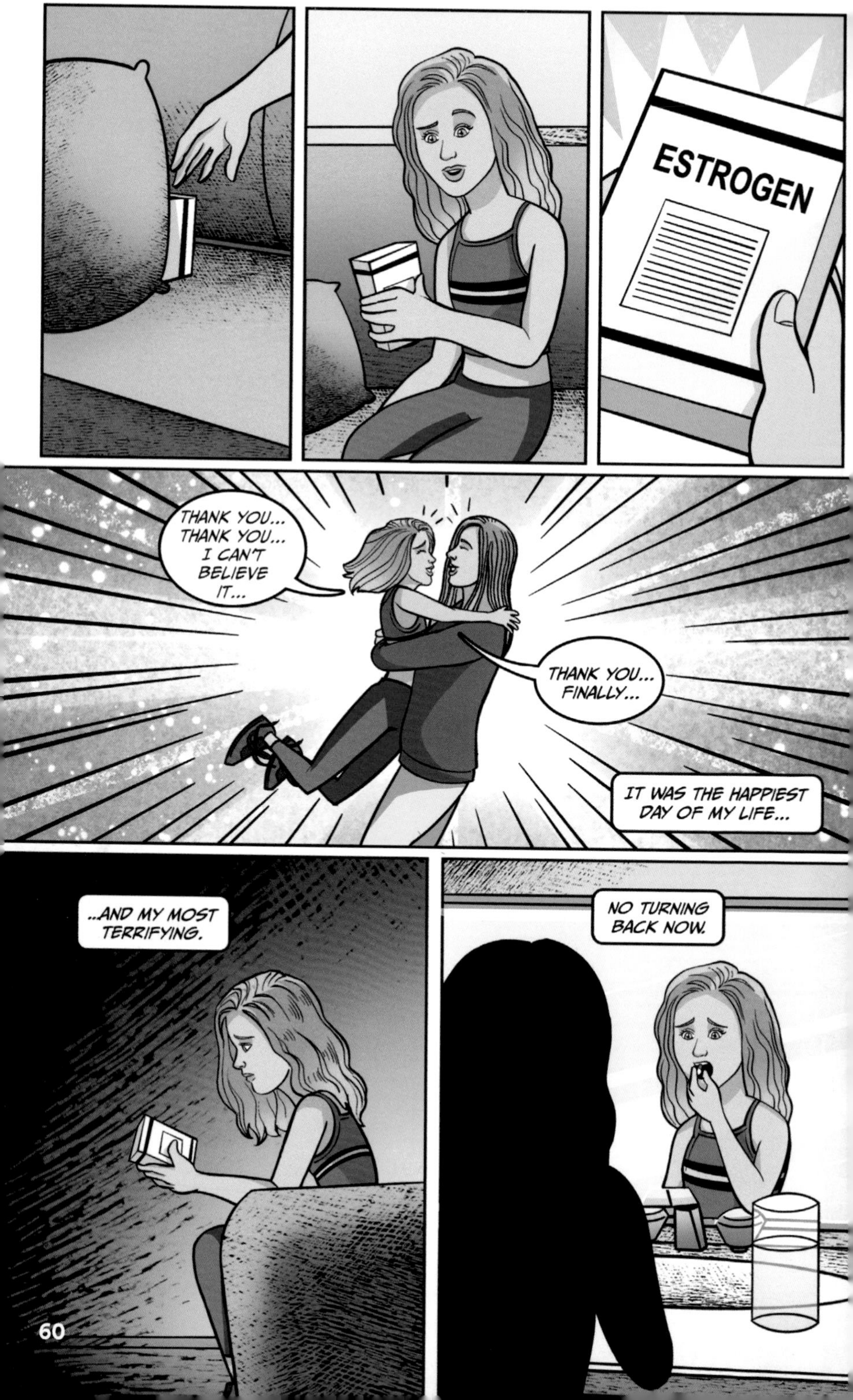
ESTROGEN
THANK YOU... THANK YOU... I CAN'T BELIEVE IT...
THANK YOU... FINALLY...
IT WAS THE HAPPIEST DAY OF MY LIFE...
...AND MY MOST TERRIFYING.
NO TURNING BACK NOW.

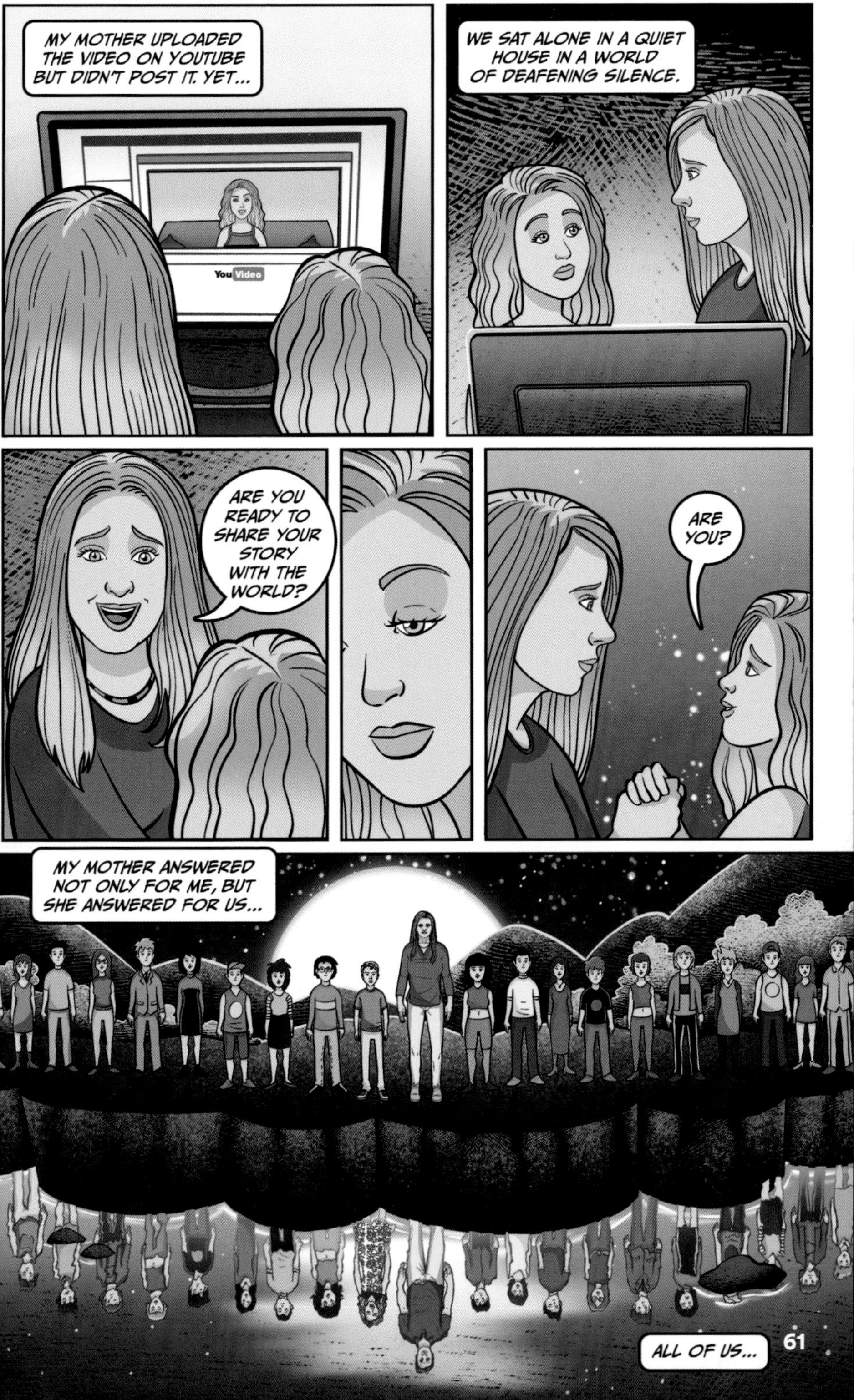

MY MOTHER UPLOADED THE VIDEO ON YOUTUBE BUT DIDN'T POST IT. YET...
You Video
WE SAT ALONE IN A QUIET HOUSE IN A WORLD OF DEAFENING SILENCE.
ARE YOU READY TO SHARE YOUR STORY WITH THE WORLD?
ARE YOU?
MY MOTHER ANSWERED NOT ONLY FOR ME, BUT SHE ANSWERED FOR US...
ALL OF US...

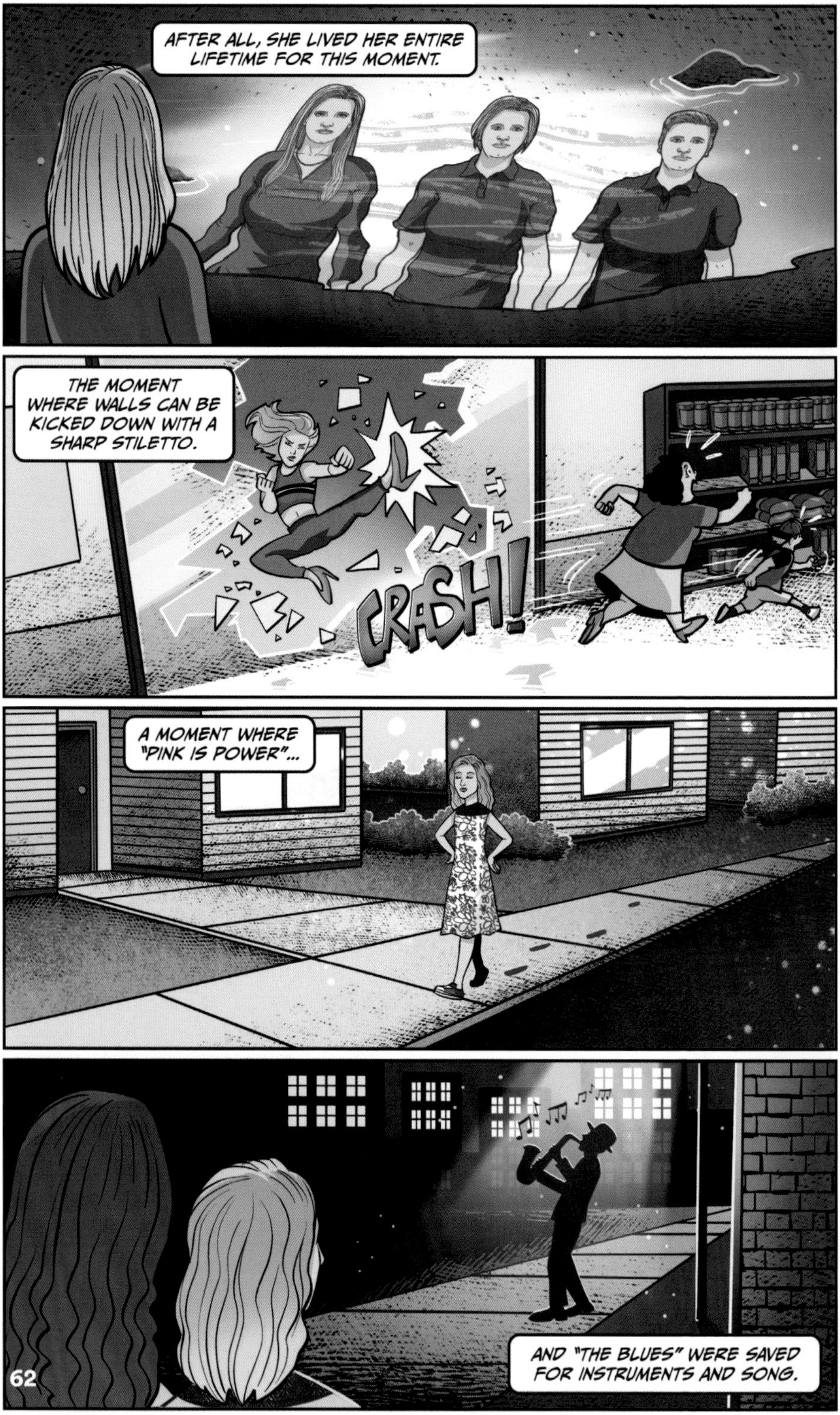
AFTER ALL, SHE LIVED HER ENTIRE LIFETIME FOR THIS MOMENT.
THE MOMENT WHERE WALLS CAN BE KICKED DOWN WITH A SHARP STILETTO.
CRASH!
A MOMENT WHERE "PINK IS POWER"...
AND "THE BLUES" WERE SAVED FOR INSTRUMENTS AND SONG.

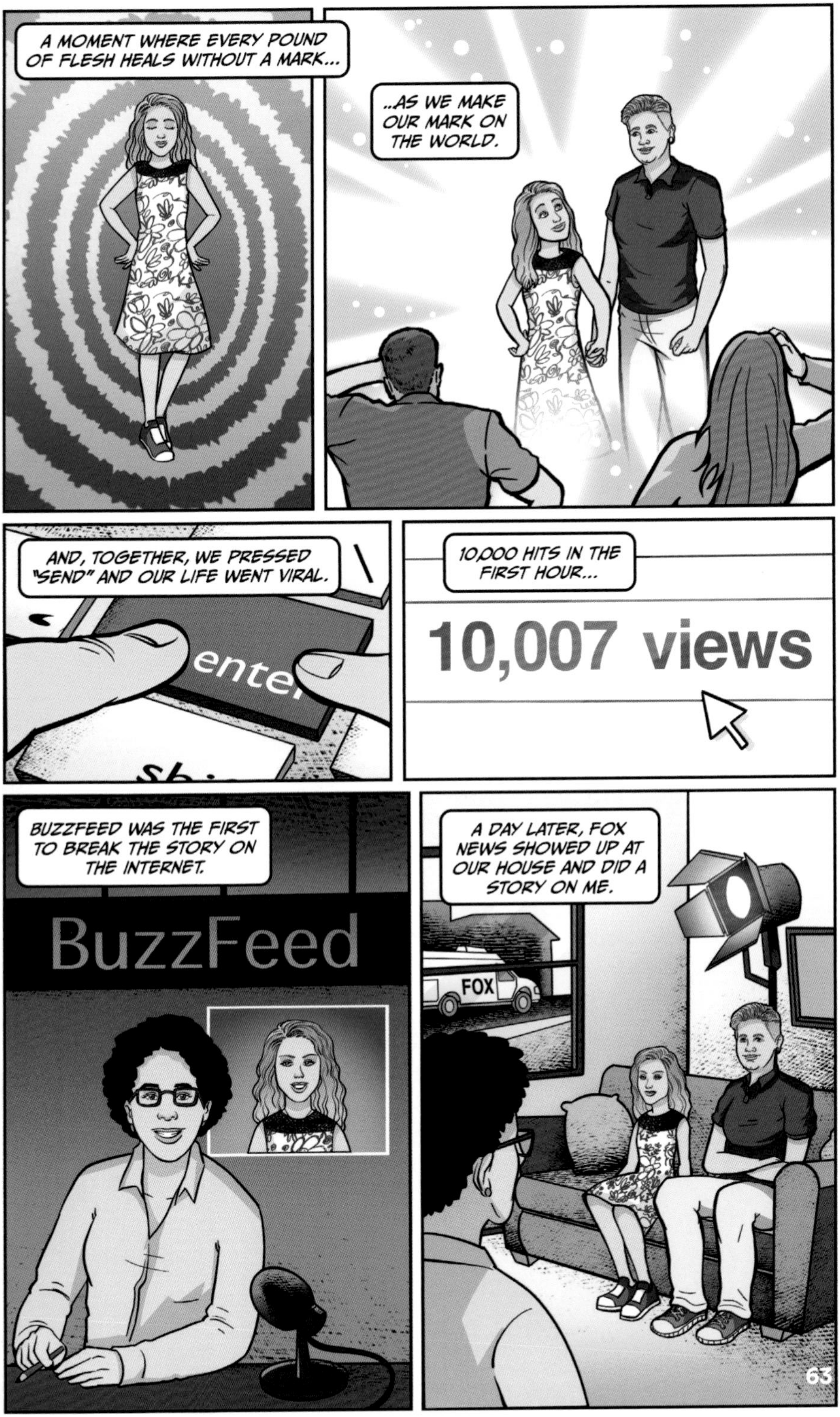

A MOMENT WHERE EVERY POUND OF FLESH HEALS WITHOUT A MARK...
...AS WE MAKE OUR MARK ON THE WORLD.
AND, TOGETHER, WE PRESSED "SEND" AND OUR LIFE WENT VIRAL.
enter
10,000 HITS IN THE FIRST HOUR...
10,007 views
BUZZFEED WAS THE FIRST TO BREAK THE STORY ON THE INTERNET.
BuzzFeed
A DAY LATER, FOX NEWS SHOWED UP AT OUR HOUSE AND DID A STORY ON ME.
FOX

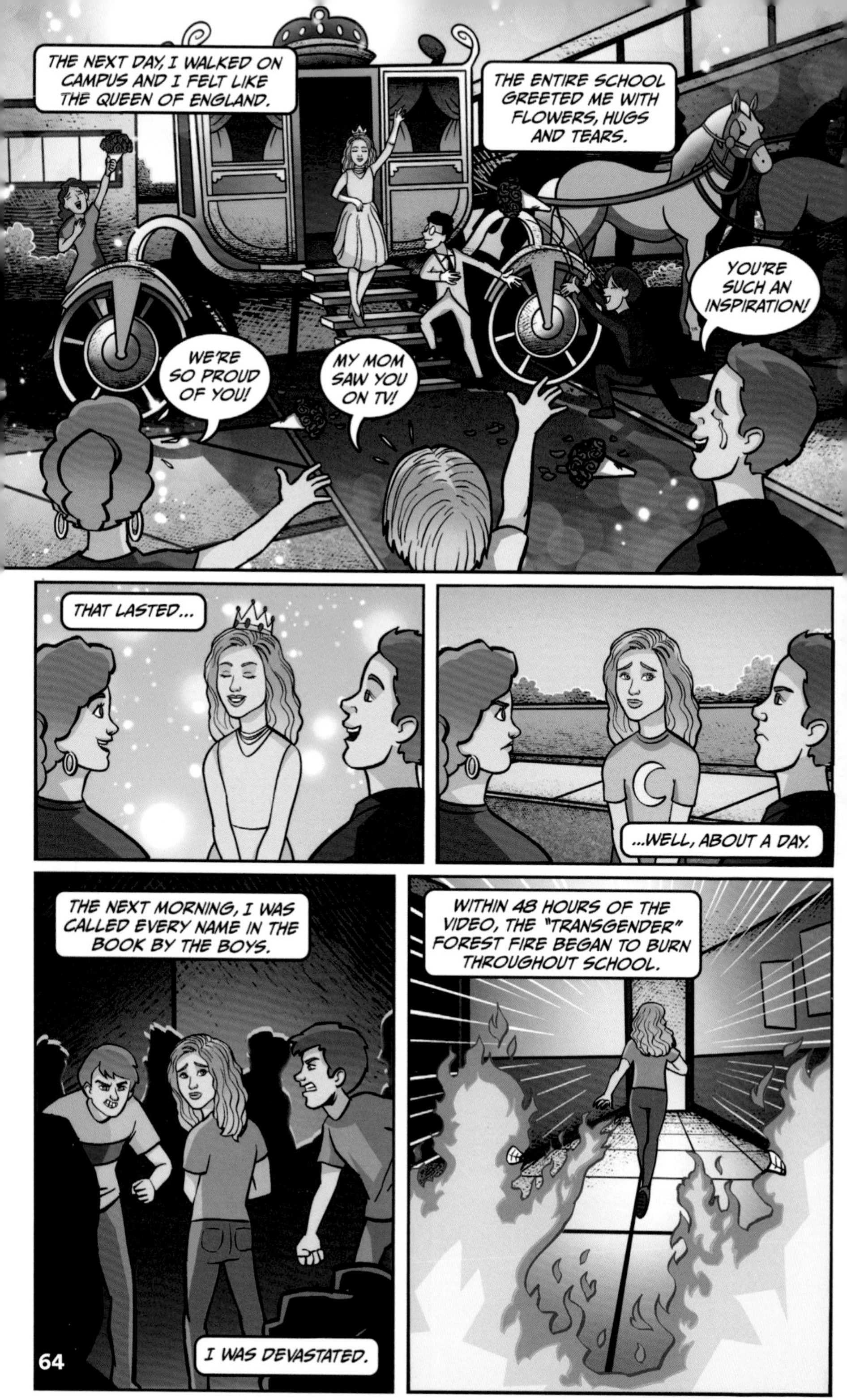

THE NEXT DAY, I WALKED ON CAMPUS AND I FELT LIKE THE QUEEN OF ENGLAND.
THE ENTIRE SCHOOL GREETED ME WITH FLOWERS, HUGS AND TEARS.
YOU'RE SUCH AN INSPIRATION!
WE'RE SO PROUD OF YOU!
MY MOM SAW YOU ON TV!
THAT LASTED...
...WELL, ABOUT A DAY.
THE NEXT MORNING, I WAS CALLED EVERY NAME IN THE BOOK BY THE BOYS.
I WAS DEVASTATED.
WITHIN 48 HOURS OF THE VIDEO, THE "TRANSGENDER" FOREST FIRE BEGAN TO BURN THROUGHOUT SCHOOL.

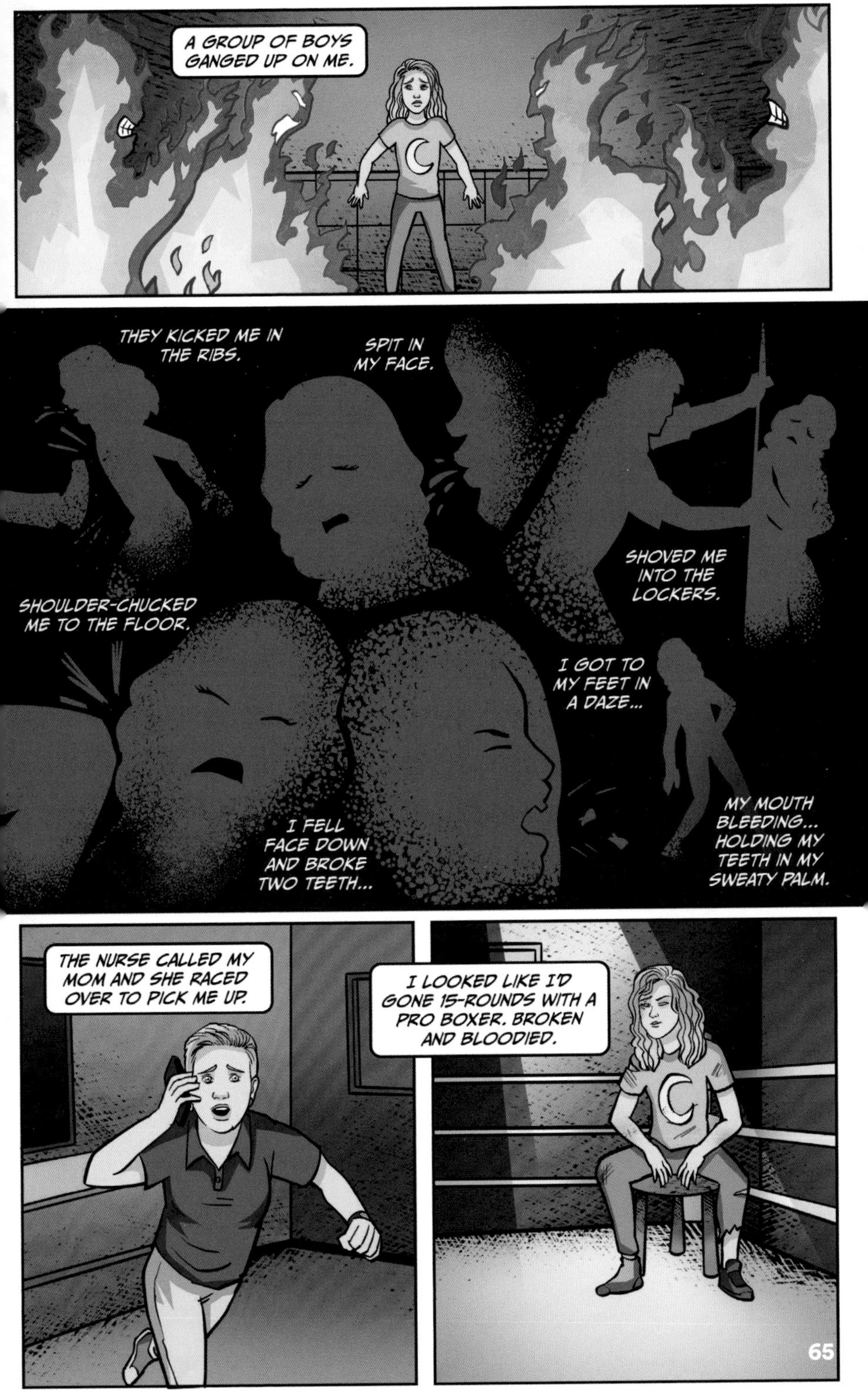
A GROUP OF BOYS GANGED UP ON ME.
THEY KICKED ME IN THE RIBS.
SPIT IN MY FACE.
SHOVED ME INTO THE LOCKERS.
SHOULDER-CHUCKED ME TO THE FLOOR.
I FELL FACE DOWN AND BROKE TWO TEETH...
I GOT TO MY FEET IN A DAZE...
MY MOUTH BLEEDING... HOLDING MY TEETH IN MY SWEATY PALM.
THE NURSE CALLED MY MOM AND SHE RACED OVER TO PICK ME UP.
I LOOKED LIKE I'D GONE 15-ROUNDS WITH A PRO BOXER. BROKEN AND BLOODIED.

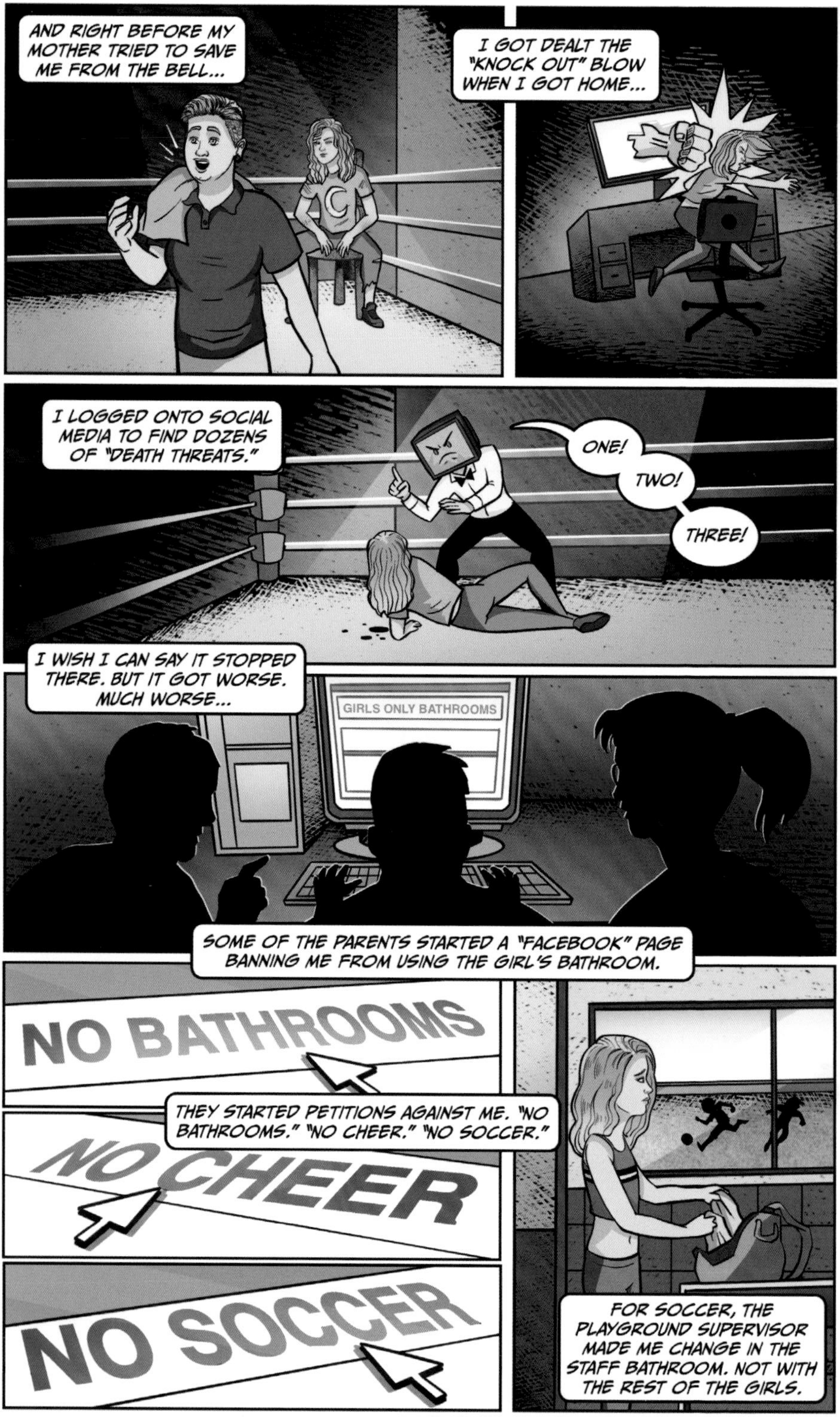

AND RIGHT BEFORE MY MOTHER TRIED TO SAVE ME FROM THE BELL...
I GOT DEALT THE "KNOCK OUT" BLOW WHEN I GOT HOME...
I LOGGED ONTO SOCIAL MEDIA TO FIND DOZENS OF "DEATH THREATS."
ONE!
TWO!
THREE!
I WISH I CAN SAY IT STOPPED THERE. BUT IT GOT WORSE. MUCH WORSE...
GIRLS ONLY BATHROOMS
SOME OF THE PARENTS STARTED A "FACEBOOK" PAGE BANNING ME FROM USING THE GIRL'S BATHROOM.
NO BATHROOMS
THEY STARTED PETITIONS AGAINST ME. "NO BATHROOMS." "NO CHEER." "NO SOCCER."
NO CHEER
NO SOCCER
FOR SOCCER, THE PLAYGROUND SUPERVISOR MADE ME CHANGE IN THE STAFF BATHROOM. NOT WITH THE REST OF THE GIRLS.

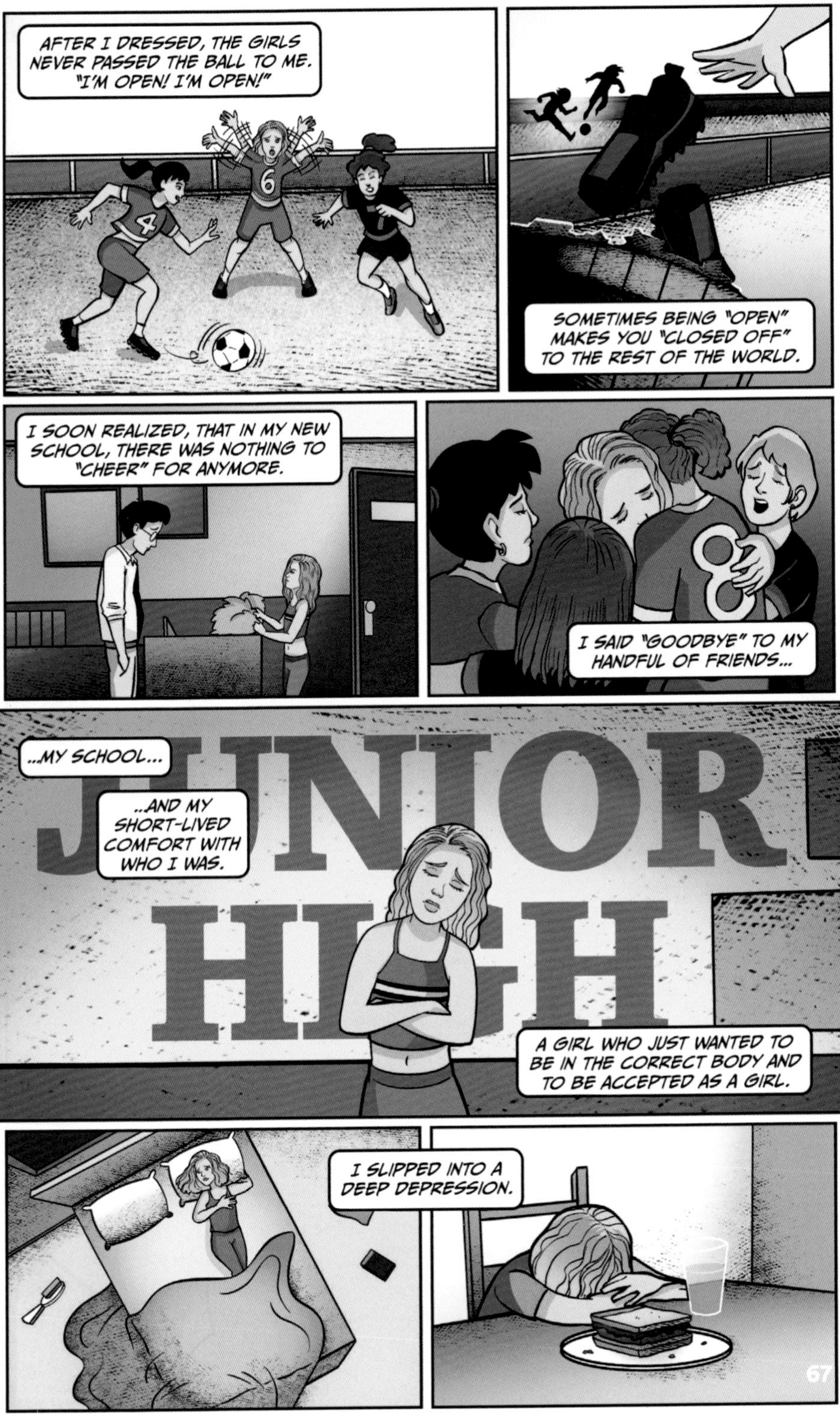
AFTER I DRESSED, THE GIRLS NEVER PASSED THE BALL TO ME. "I'M OPEN! I'M OPEN!"
SOMETIMES BEING "OPEN" MAKES YOU "CLOSED OFF" TO THE REST OF THE WORLD.
I SOON REALIZED, THAT IN MY NEW SCHOOL, THERE WAS NOTHING TO "CHEER" FOR ANYMORE.
I SAID "GOODBYE" TO MY HANDFUL OF FRIENDS...
...MY SCHOOL...
JUNIOR HIGH
...AND MY SHORT-LIVED COMFORT WITH WHO I WAS.
A GIRL WHO JUST WANTED TO BE IN THE CORRECT BODY AND TO BE ACCEPTED AS A GIRL.
I SLIPPED INTO A DEEP DEPRESSION.

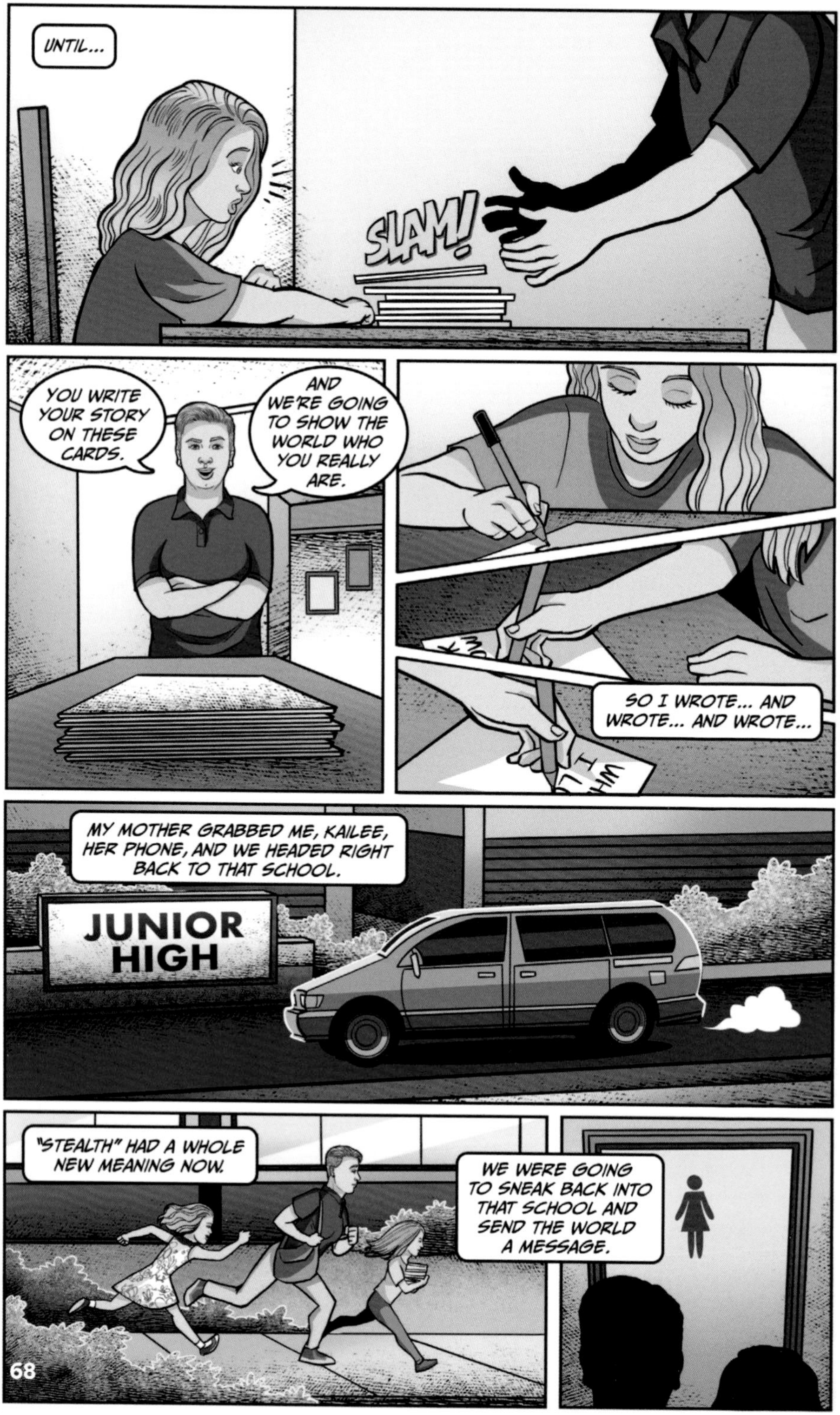
UNTIL...
SLAM!
YOU WRITE YOUR STORY ON THESE CARDS.
AND WE'RE GOING TO SHOW THE WORLD WHO YOU REALLY ARE.
SO I WROTE... AND WROTE... AND WROTE...
MY MOTHER GRABBED ME, KAILEE, HER PHONE, AND WE HEADED RIGHT BACK TO THAT SCHOOL.
JUNIOR HIGH
"STEALTH" HAD A WHOLE NEW MEANING NOW.
WE WERE GOING TO SNEAK BACK INTO THAT SCHOOL AND SEND THE WORLD A MESSAGE.

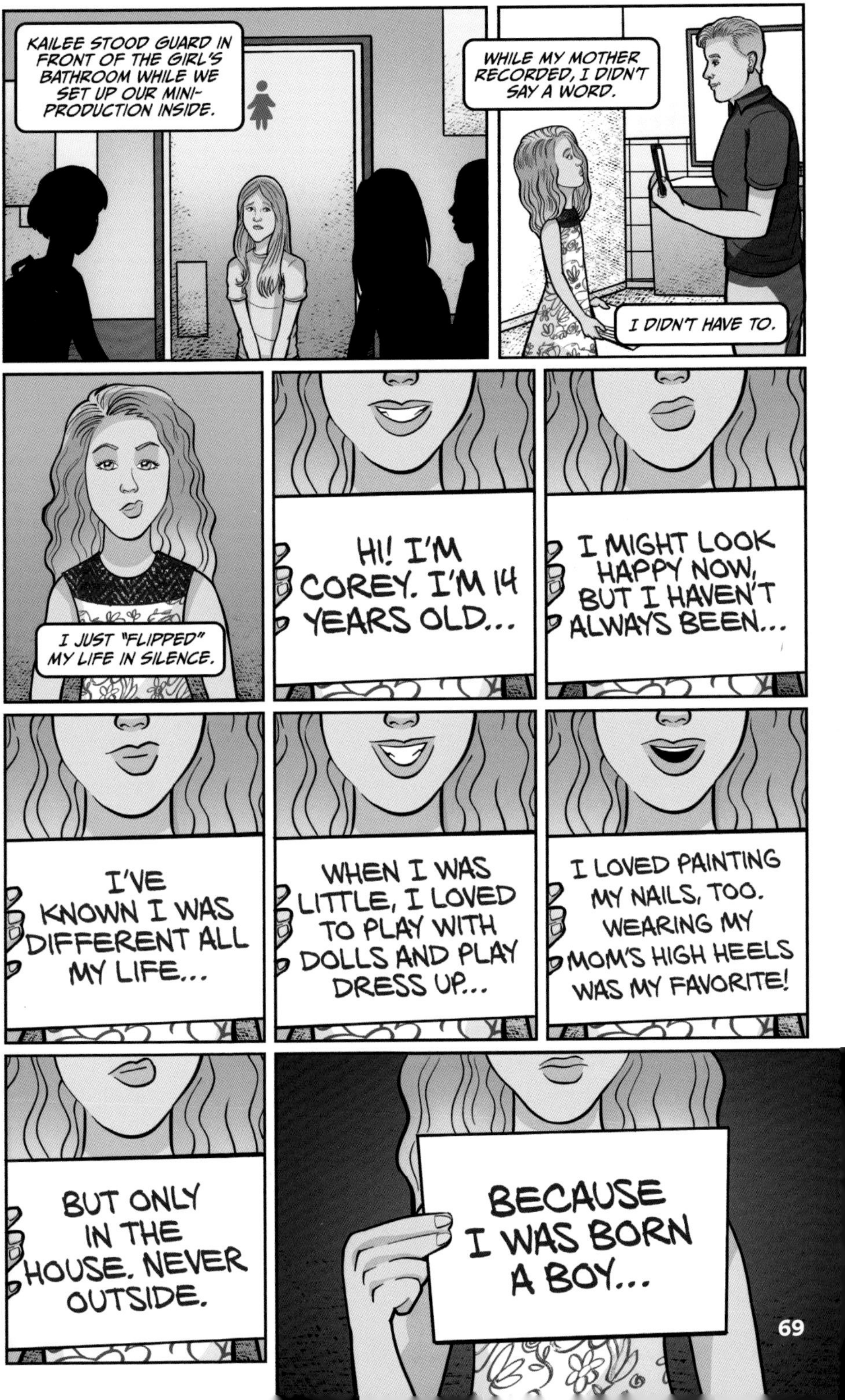

KAILEE STOOD GUARD IN FRONT OF THE GIRL'S BATHROOM WHILE WE SET UP OUR MINI-PRODUCTION INSIDE.
WHILE MY MOTHER RECORDED, I DIDN'T SAY A WORD.
I DIDN'T HAVE TO.
I JUST "FLIPPED" MY LIFE IN SILENCE.
HI! I'M COREY. I'M 14 YEARS OLD...
I MIGHT LOOK HAPPY NOW, BUT I HAVEN'T ALWAYS BEEN...
I'VE KNOWN I WAS DIFFERENT ALL MY LIFE...
WHEN I WAS LITTLE, I LOVED TO PLAY WITH DOLLS AND PLAY DRESS UP...
I LOVED PAINTING MY NAILS, TOO. WEARING MY MOM'S HIGH HEELS WAS MY FAVORITE!
BUT ONLY IN THE HOUSE. NEVER OUTSIDE.
BECAUSE I WAS BORN A BOY...

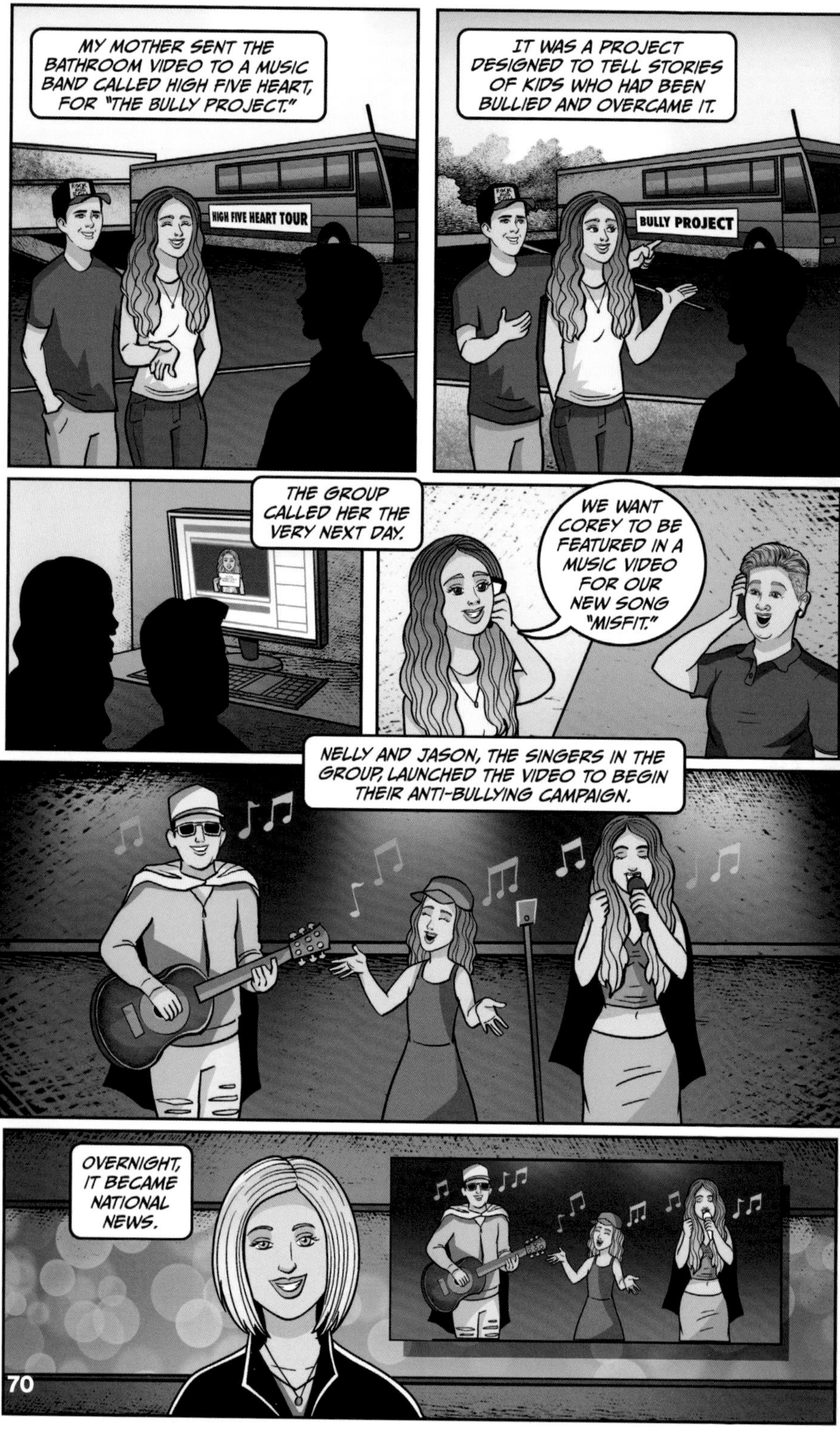

MY MOTHER SENT THE BATHROOM VIDEO TO A MUSIC BAND CALLED HIGH FIVE HEART, FOR "THE BULLY PROJECT."
HIGH FIVE HEART TOUR
IT WAS A PROJECT DESIGNED TO TELL STORIES OF KIDS WHO HAD BEEN BULLIED AND OVERCAME IT.
BULLY PROJECT
THE GROUP CALLED HER THE VERY NEXT DAY.
WE WANT COREY TO BE FEATURED IN A MUSIC VIDEO FOR OUR NEW SONG "MISFIT."
NELLY AND JASON, THE SINGERS IN THE GROUP, LAUNCHED THE VIDEO TO BEGIN THEIR ANTI-BULLYING CAMPAIGN.
OVERNIGHT, IT BECAME NATIONAL NEWS.

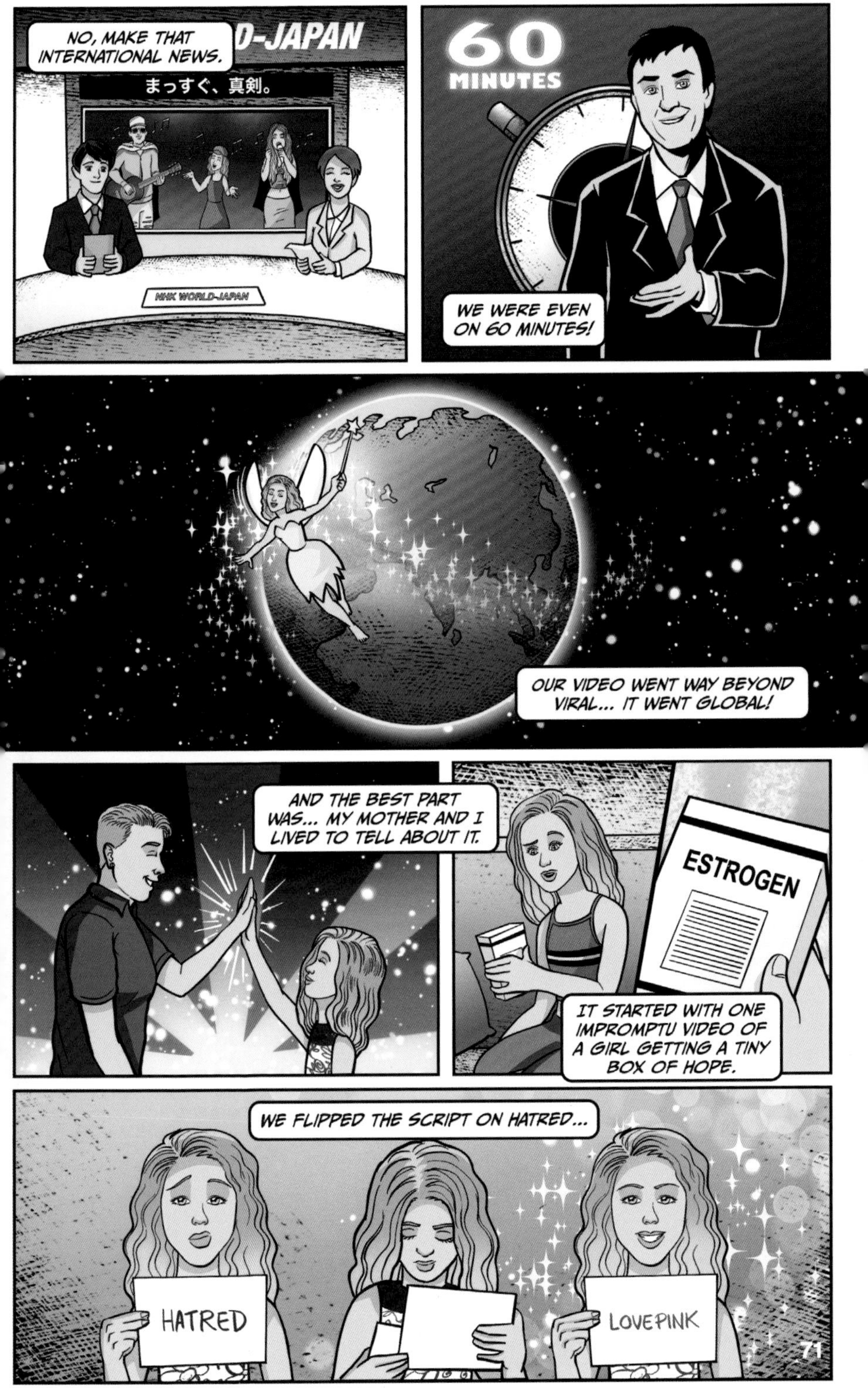

NO, MAKE THAT INTERNATIONAL NEWS.
D-JAPAN
まっすぐ、真剣。
NHK WORLD-JAPAN
60 MINUTES
WE WERE EVEN ON 60 MINUTES!
OUR VIDEO WENT WAY BEYOND VIRAL... IT WENT GLOBAL!
AND THE BEST PART WAS... MY MOTHER AND I LIVED TO TELL ABOUT IT.
ESTROGEN
IT STARTED WITH ONE IMPROMPTU VIDEO OF A GIRL GETTING A TINY BOX OF HOPE.
WE FLIPPED THE SCRIPT ON HATRED...
HATRED
LOVEPINK

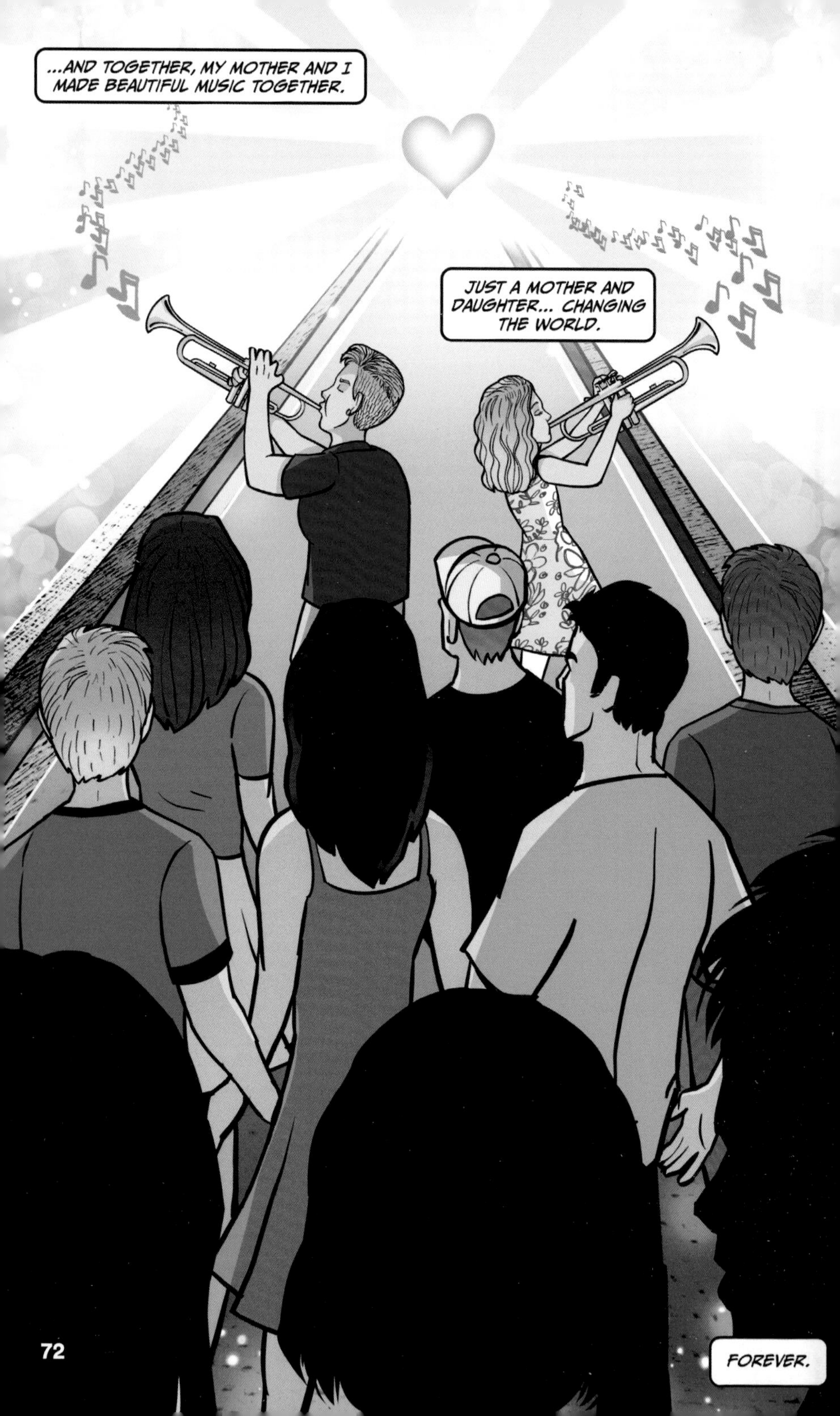
...AND TOGETHER, MY MOTHER AND I MADE BEAUTIFUL MUSIC TOGETHER.
JUST A MOTHER AND DAUGHTER... CHANGING THE WORLD.
FOREVER.

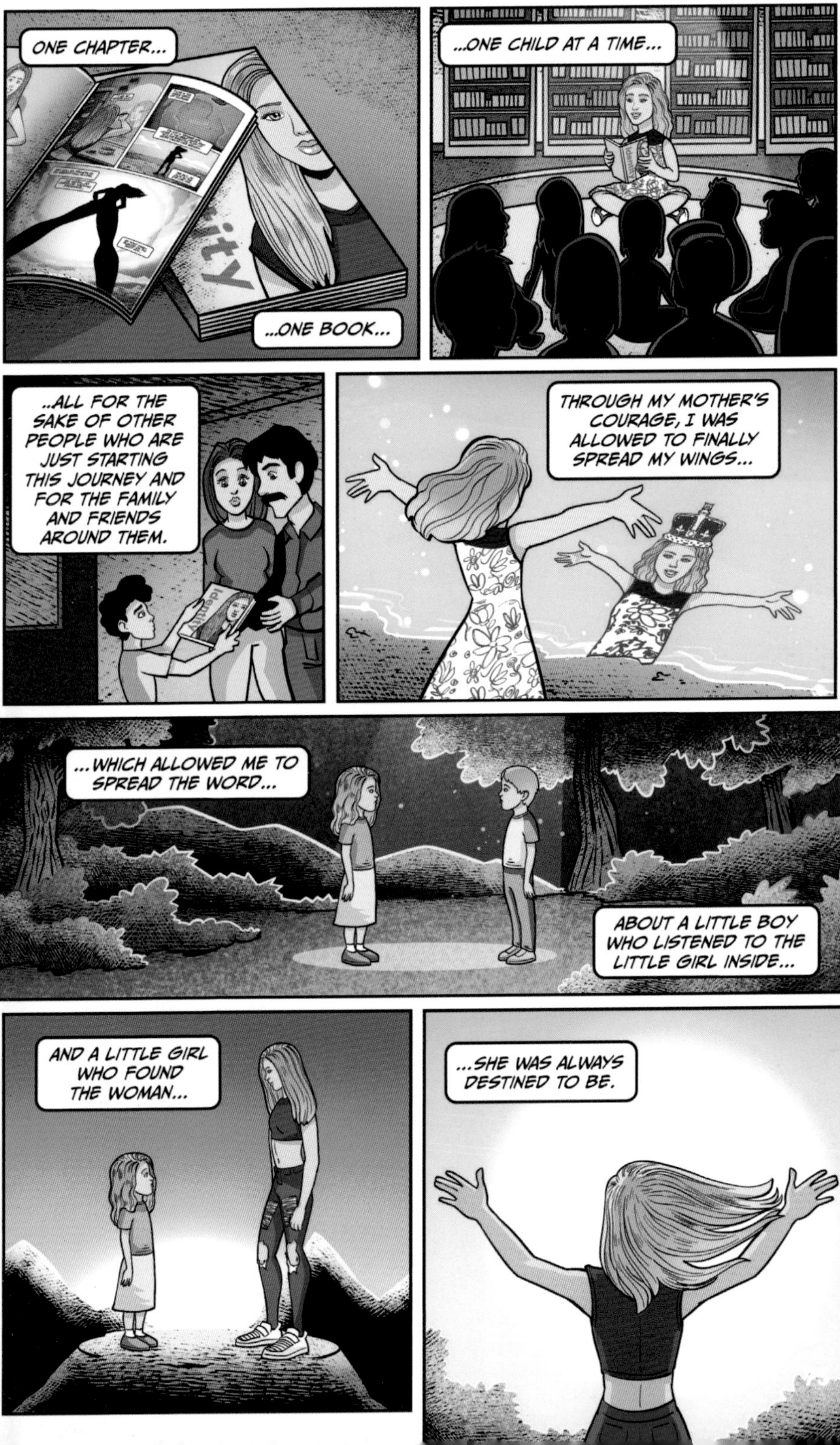
ONE CHAPTER...
...ONE BOOK...
...ONE CHILD AT A TIME...
..ALL FOR THE SAKE OF OTHER PEOPLE WHO ARE JUST STARTING THIS JOURNEY AND FOR THE FAMILY AND FRIENDS AROUND THEM.
THROUGH MY MOTHER'S COURAGE, I WAS ALLOWED TO FINALLY SPREAD MY WINGS...
...WHICH ALLOWED ME TO SPREAD THE WORD...
ABOUT A LITTLE BOY WHO LISTENED TO THE LITTLE GIRL INSIDE...
AND A LITTLE GIRL WHO FOUND THE WOMAN...
...SHE WAS ALWAYS DESTINED TO BE.

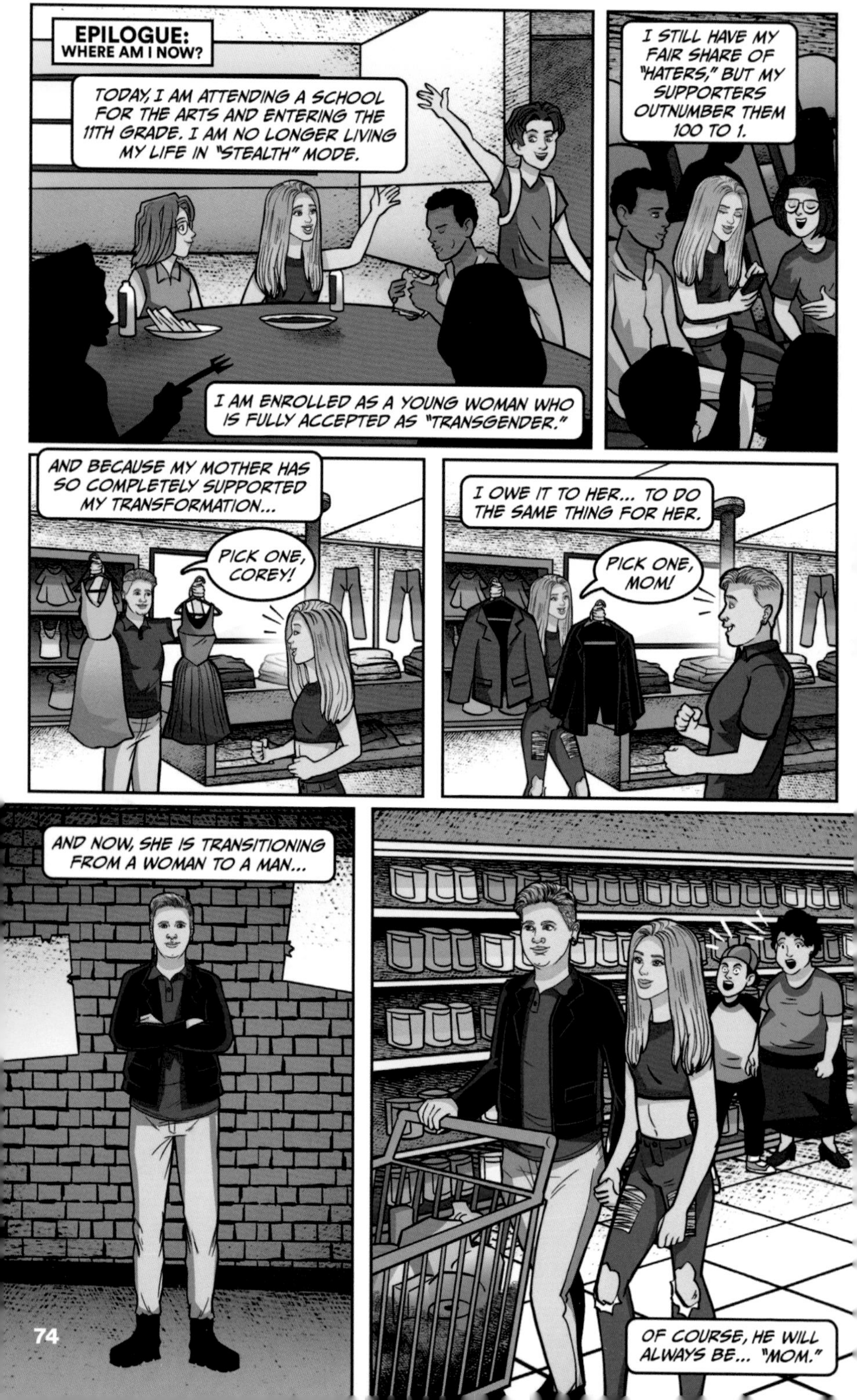

EPILOGUE:
WHERE AM I NOW?
TODAY, I AM ATTENDING A SCHOOL FOR THE ARTS AND ENTERING THE 11TH GRADE. I AM NO LONGER LIVING MY LIFE IN "STEALTH" MODE.
I AM ENROLLED AS A YOUNG WOMAN WHO IS FULLY ACCEPTED AS "TRANSGENDER."
I STILL HAVE MY FAIR SHARE OF "HATERS," BUT MY SUPPORTERS OUTNUMBER THEM 100 TO 1.
AND BECAUSE MY MOTHER HAS SO COMPLETELY SUPPORTED MY TRANSFORMATION...
PICK ONE, COREY!
I OWE IT TO HER... TO DO THE SAME THING FOR HER.
PICK ONE, MOM!
AND NOW, SHE IS TRANSITIONING FROM A WOMAN TO A MAN...
OF COURSE, HE WILL ALWAYS BE... "MOM."

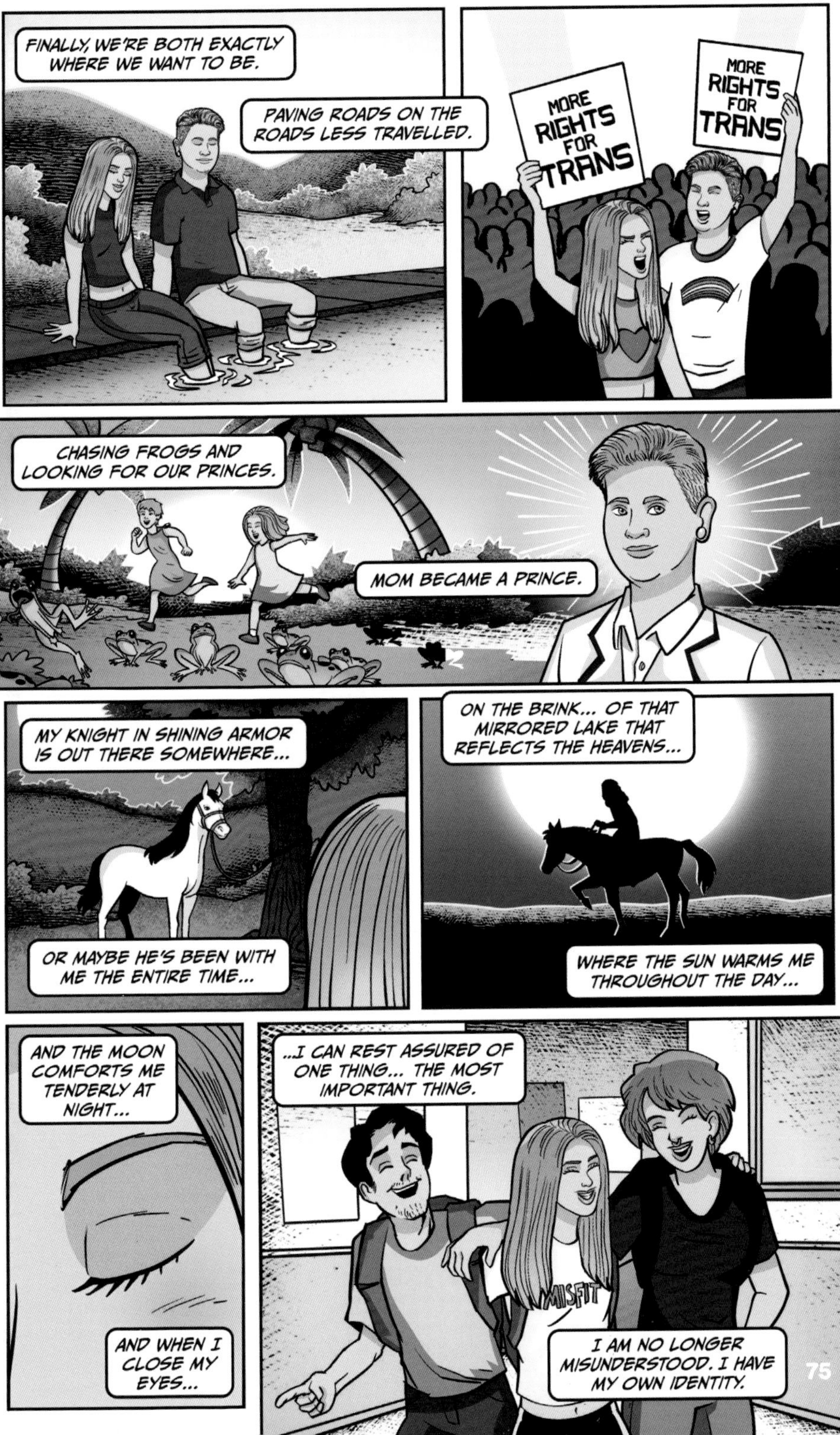

FINALLY, WE'RE BOTH EXACTLY WHERE WE WANT TO BE.
PAVING ROADS ON THE ROADS LESS TRAVELLED.
MORE RIGHTS FOR TRANS
MORE RIGHTS FOR TRANS
CHASING FROGS AND LOOKING FOR OUR PRINCES.
MOM BECAME A PRINCE.
MY KNIGHT IN SHINING ARMOR IS OUT THERE SOMEWHERE...
OR MAYBE HE'S BEEN WITH ME THE ENTIRE TIME...
ON THE BRINK... OF THAT MIRRORED LAKE THAT REFLECTS THE HEAVENS...
WHERE THE SUN WARMS ME THROUGHOUT THE DAY...
AND THE MOON COMFORTS ME TENDERLY AT NIGHT...
AND WHEN I CLOSE MY EYES...
...I CAN REST ASSURED OF ONE THING... THE MOST IMPORTANT THING.
MISFIT
I AM NO LONGER MISUNDERSTOOD. I HAVE MY OWN IDENTITY.

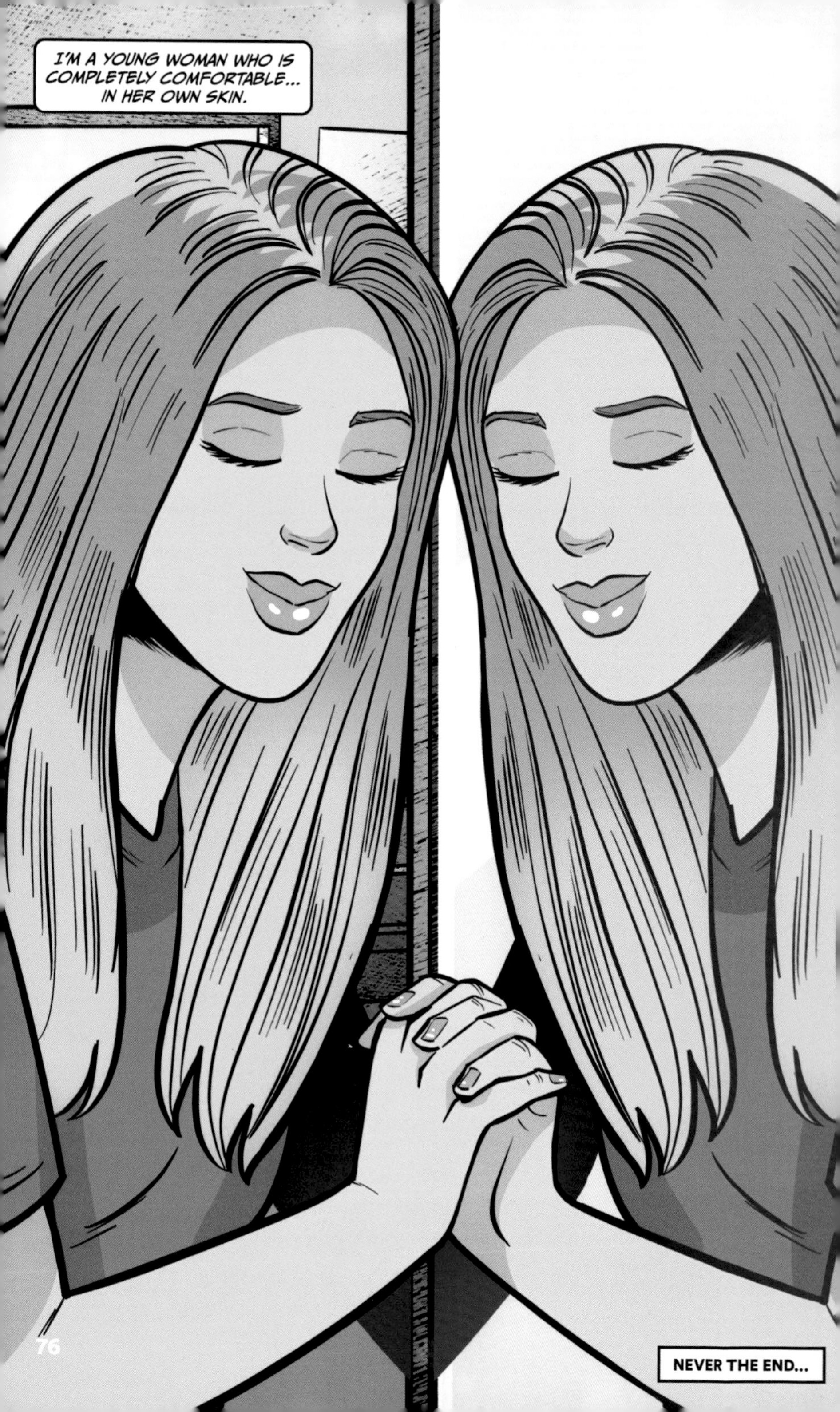
I'M A YOUNG WOMAN WHO IS COMPLETELY COMFORTABLE... IN HER OWN SKIN.
NEVER THE END...

ABOUT THE AUTHOR

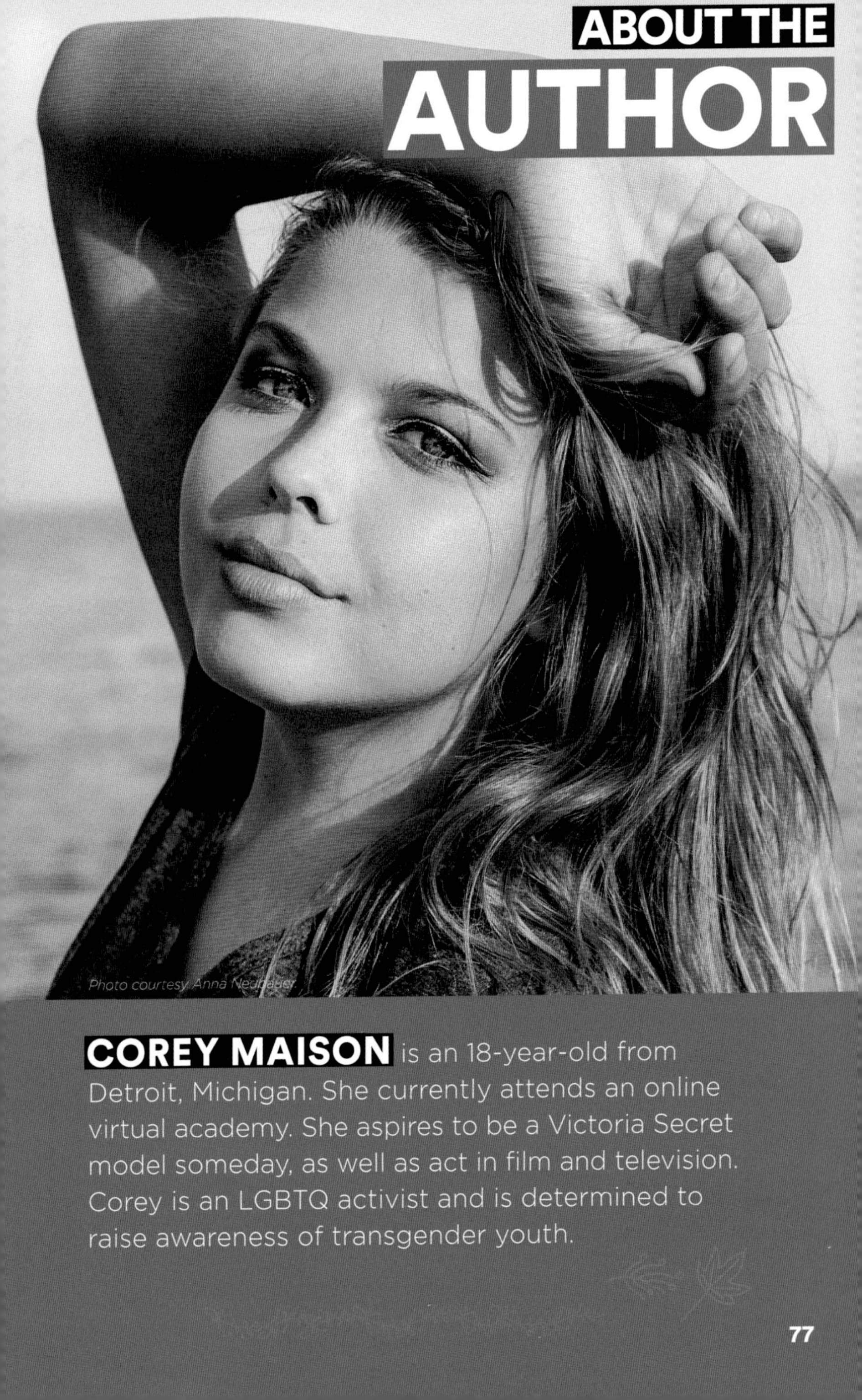

Photo courtesy Anna Neubauer

COREY MAISON is an 18-year-old from Detroit, Michigan. She currently attends an online virtual academy. She aspires to be a Victoria Secret model someday, as well as act in film and television. Corey is an LGBTQ activist and is determined to raise awareness of transgender youth.

COREY...

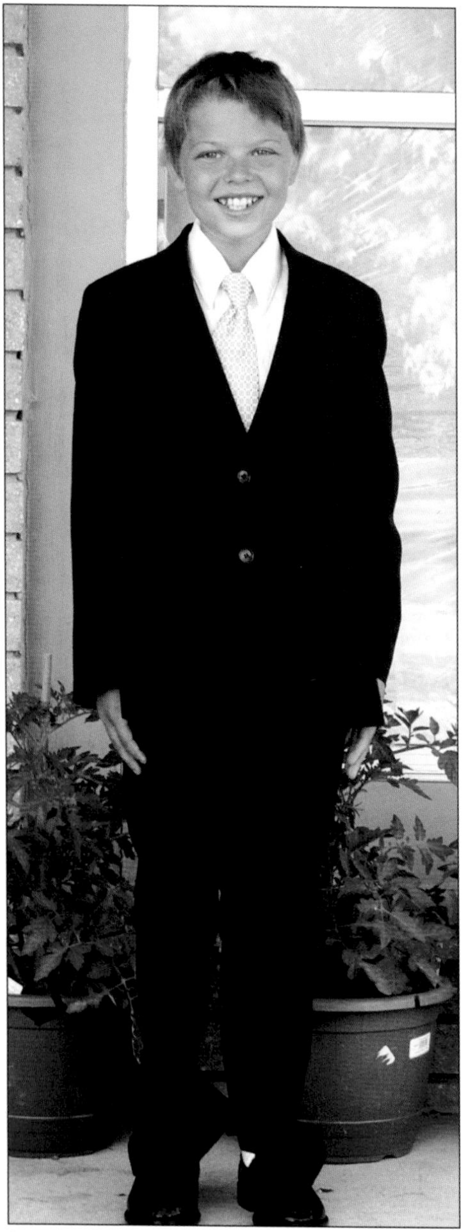

I was ten years old, headed to fifth grade graduation. I began my transition less than a week later.

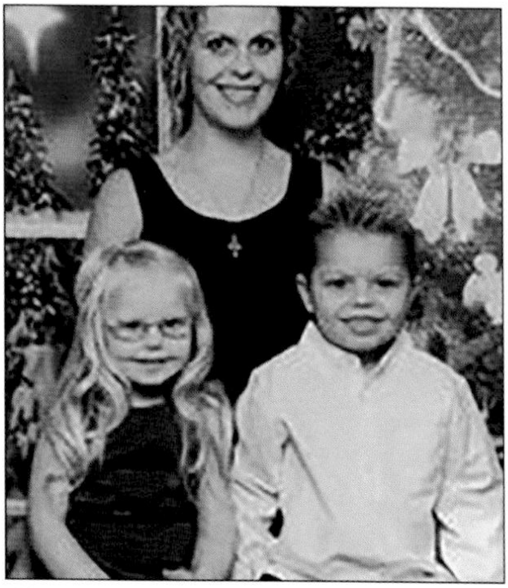

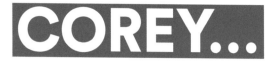

Christmas pictures with my mom and sister when it was just us.

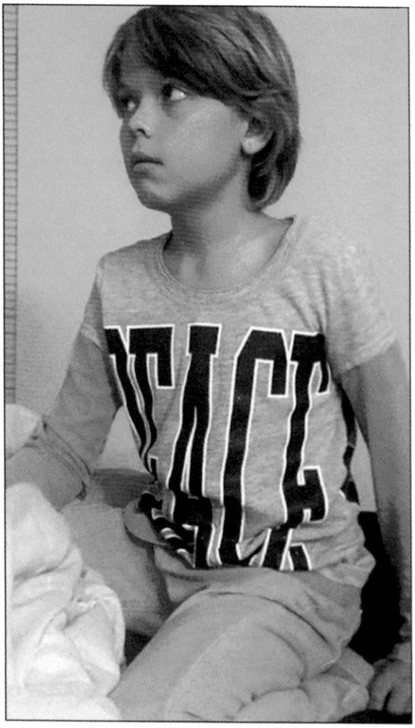

The first outfit my mom let me pick out myself, also the first time I wore PINK!

...COREY

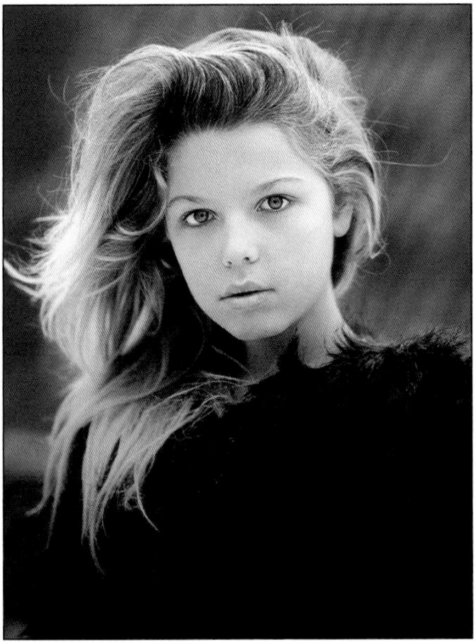

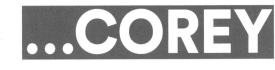

This photo was taken on a rooftop. I felt like I was flying as free as a bird wearing the feathers. *Photo courtesy Anna Neubauer.*

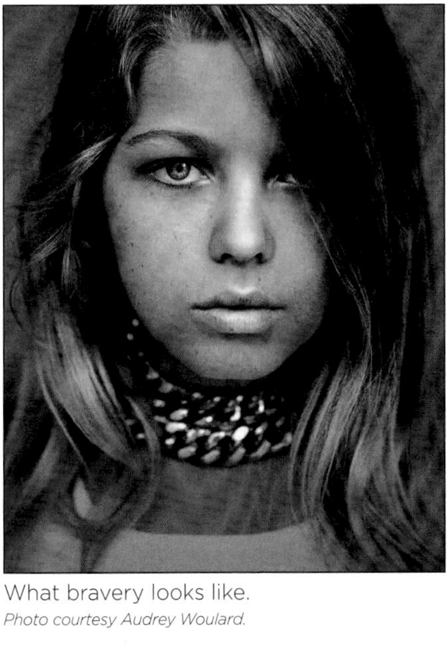

What bravery looks like.
Photo courtesy Audrey Woulard.

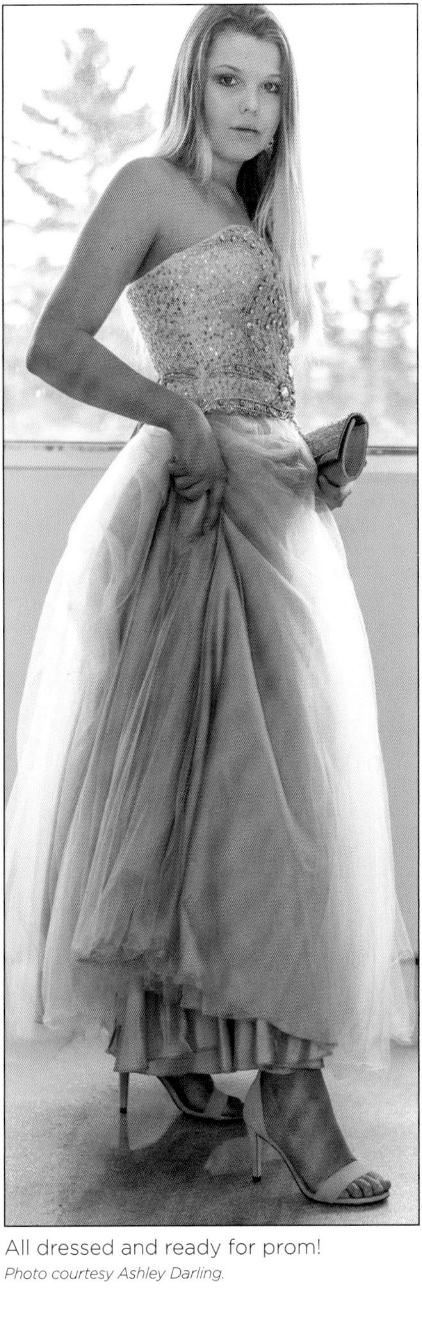

All dressed and ready for prom!
Photo courtesy Ashley Darling.

COREY...

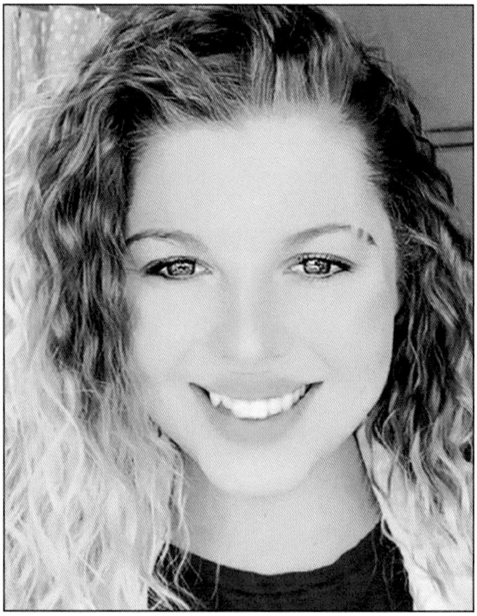

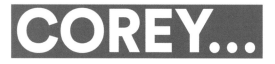

I love the quote: "Use your smile to change the world, don't let the world change your smile."

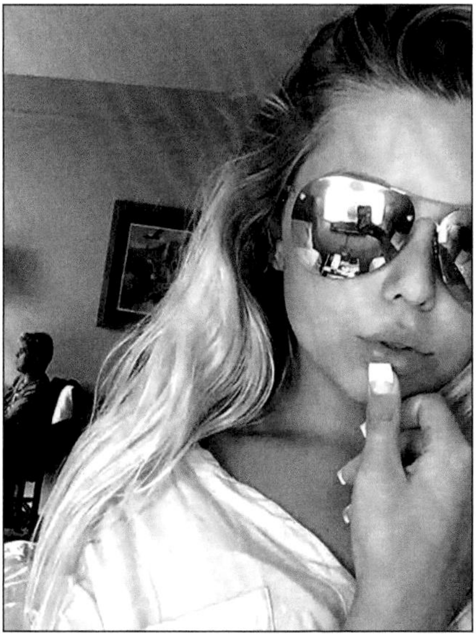

Feeling myself. Confidence is key.

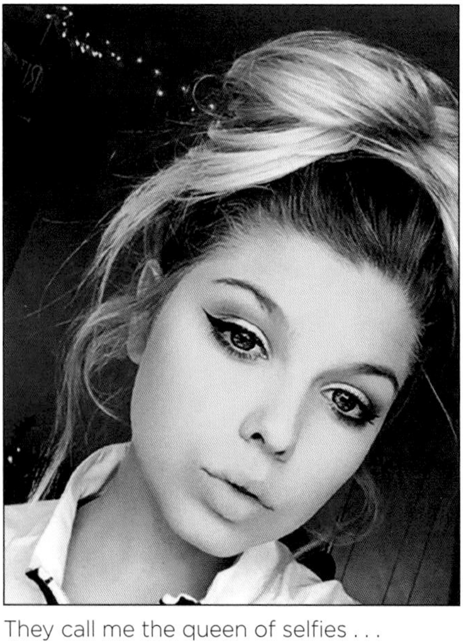

They call me the queen of selfies . . . but hair and makeup on point!

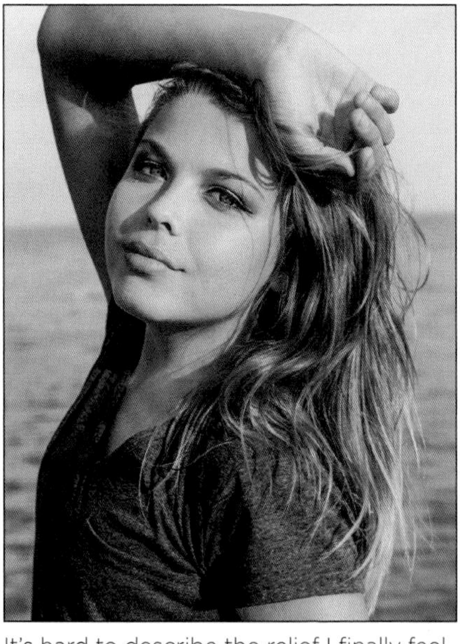

It's hard to describe the relief I finally feel after transitioning. This is ME.

Photo courtesy Anna Neubauer.

TAKE 5!
FIVE PARENT TAKE-AWAYS ABOUT TRANSITIONING

DR. POWERS is a Board Certified Family Medicine Physician who has a practice in Farmington Hills, Michigan, specializing in care of LGBT people. He regularly lectures around the country about transgender medicine.

TRANSGENDER CHILDREN OCCUR ABOUT AS OFTEN IN THE US POPULATION AS RED HAIR OR GREEN EYES.

Approximately 1.5% of kids identify as transgender, but fear of rejection leads many to hide their identity. It's important for adults in the child's life to offer support and affirmation of their identity in order to avoid severe psychological harm. Around 40% of transgender teens report having attempted suicide at least once. A support system that affirms a child's gender identity is crucial as they continue to develop and grow.

SOMETIMES GENDER DYSPHORIA IS DUE TO AN UNDERLYING MEDICAL CONDITION.

There are a number of medical conditions which can cause a person to develop gender dysphoria. Every child who presents with gender dysphoria should undergo a full medical examination.

A TRANSGENDER IDENTITY IS VALID REGARDLESS OF MEDICAL TREATMENT.

Although there shouldn't be a rush to transition with hormones, in some cases medical interventions should be started immediately. The changes caused by going through what feels like the "wrong" puberty are not easily reversed and can greatly increase dysphoria and depression. Children who express a gender identity that does not match the sex they were assigned at birth can be placed on puberty blockers. These medications are used to temporarily pause puberty to allow time for psychological evaluation and development. When the child reaches the age of puberty, or when they are considered to be a good (or poor) candidate for hormones, these puberty blockers can be stopped. This allows puberty to start normally or be induced with different hormones. Not every transgender person needs or even wants surgery or hormones.

THE MEDICAL COMMUNITY DOES NOT SUPPORT OR EVEN CONDONE IRREVERSIBLE TRANSGENDER SURGERIES ON CHILDREN.

Except in extremely rare cases, gender affirming surgeries are almost never performed on minors. A watch, wait, and affirm their identity strategy has been shown to have the lowest complications while also reducing the risk of suicide and self-harm.

BEING TRANSGENDER IS NOT THE SAME AS BEING GAY.

Sexual orientation and gender identity are not the same. Some transgender youth will be heterosexual, some will not. Sometimes their sexual orientation may change if they start hormone therapy. If a transgender boy (assigned female at birth) is attracted only to females, he is considered heterosexual. If attracted only to men, he is considered homosexual. It's important to recognize that gender identity and sexual orientation are not the same and vary from person to person.

THE STORY DOESN'T END HERE...

VISIT
ZUIKERPRESS.COM

... to learn more about Corey's story, see behind-the-scenes videos of Corey and her family.

Our **WEBSITE** is another resource to help our readers deal with the issues that they face every day. Log on to find advice from experts, links to helpful organizations and literature, and more real-life experiences from young people just like you.

Spotlighting young writers with heartfelt stories that enlighten and inspire.

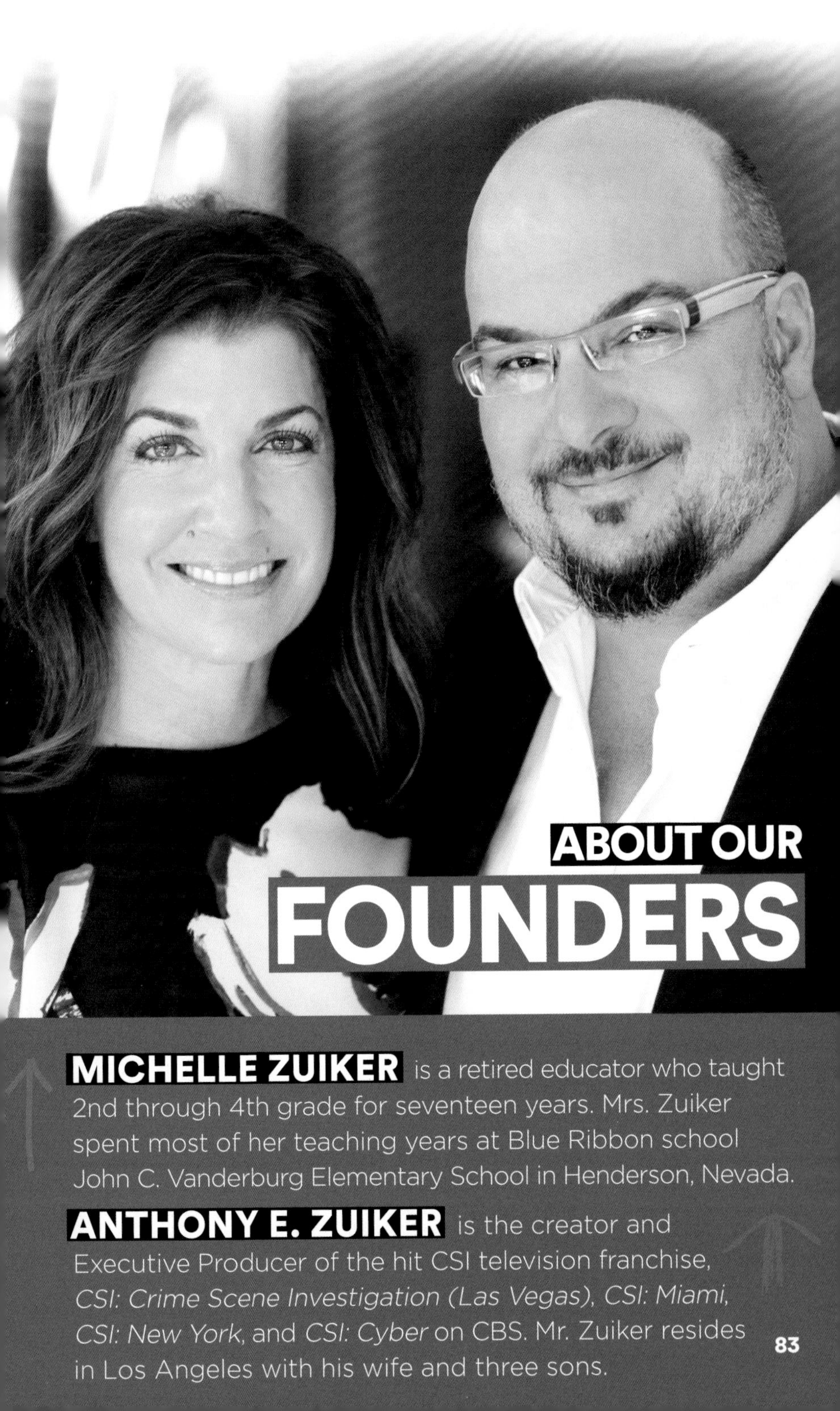

ABOUT OUR FOUNDERS

MICHELLE ZUIKER is a retired educator who taught 2nd through 4th grade for seventeen years. Mrs. Zuiker spent most of her teaching years at Blue Ribbon school John C. Vanderburg Elementary School in Henderson, Nevada.

ANTHONY E. ZUIKER is the creator and Executive Producer of the hit CSI television franchise, *CSI: Crime Scene Investigation (Las Vegas)*, *CSI: Miami*, *CSI: New York*, and *CSI: Cyber* on CBS. Mr. Zuiker resides in Los Angeles with his wife and three sons.

AVAILABLE NOW continued...

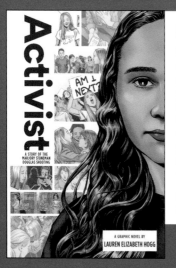

ACTIVIST: A STORY OF THE MARJORY STONEMAN DOUGLAS SHOOTING

The horrific school shooting in Parkland, Florida, led many survivors, including Lauren Hogg and her brother David, to become activists to promote rational gun safety laws.

"A great book written for teens by a peer that shows how, out of tragedy, strength and hope can grow."
—Booklist

ISBN: 978-1-947378-21-6 HARDCOVER $12.99
ISBN: 978-1-947378-23-0 EBOOK $7.99

BROTHER: A STORY OF AUTISM

Growing up with a brother who has autism can be confusing and frustrating, as Bridget tells us in her book about Carlton, but it is ultimately rewarding for both of them.

"[Brother is] the perfect answer to those who wonder what it is like to have a sibling on the spectrum."—Kirkus

ISBN: 978-1-947378-08-7 HARDCOVER $12.99
ISBN: 978-1-947378-10-0 EBOOK $7.99

ZUIKERPRESS.COM

GOODBYE: A STORY OF SUICIDE

When Hailee was twelve years old, the bullying began. Days after her thirteenth birthday, she had taken her own life.

ISBN: 978-1-947378-27-8 HARDCOVER $12.99
ISBN: 978-1-947378-29-2 EBOOK $7.99

COMING SPRING 2021

ONE SHOT: A STORY OF BULLYING
BY ALEX KARL BRUORTON

A gripping story of a boy who suffers from CLOVES syndrome.

ISBN 978-1-947378-30-8 HARDCOVER $12.99
ISBN 978-1-947378-32-2 EBOOK $7.99

Zuiker Press

ZUIKERPRESS.COM